P9-BJY-290

ATLANTA REVIEW

SLOVAKIA

International Section Edited by

Nina Varon & Miriam Margala

Spring/Summer 2024

ATLANTA REVIEW

at the Georgia Institute of Technology

Co-Editor	**Karen Head**
Co-Editor	**JC Reilly**
Editor Emeritus	**Dan Veach**
Editorial Board	**Victoria Chang**
	Travis Denton
Senior Reader	Whitney Cooper
Senior Reader	Rebekah Greene
Senior Reader	Anne Leigh Parrish
Senior Reader	Agnes Vojta

Reading Interns

Avery Cole, Charlotte Nagel, and Kat Petty

Atlanta Review logo designed by Malone Tumlin Davidson

Visit our website: **www.atlantareview.com**
Atlanta Review appears in May and December.
Subscriptions are $20 ($25 Int.) a year.

Available in full text in Ebsco, ProQuest, & Cengage databases.
Subscriptions are available through Ebsco, Blackwell, and Swets.

Submission Guidelines:
Up to five unpublished poems, without identifying information on any poem.
Postal submissions **must** include a SASE & cover letter with contact informa-
tion and a list of poem titles submitted. For more specific info, visit our website.
Or submit online at https://atlantareview.submittable.com/submit

Please send postal mail submissions and subscription requests to:
ATLANTA REVIEW
686 Cherry St. NW
Atlanta GA 30332-0161
© Copyright 2024 by *Atlanta Review*.   ISSN 1073-9696

Atlanta Review is a nonprofit literary journal.
Contributions are tax-deductible.

WELCOME

When Dan Veach asked me to consider taking on the editorship of *Atlanta Review*, I knew it would be a passion project that bring joy in ways I couldn't imagine. And then, in the middle of what would be my tenure of editorship, the world shut down. The passion for bringing poetry to people became more important than it had ever been—it was a comfort for us all, and a tie that bound us when we felt so separated from one another. It has been an honor to be trusted with so many wonderful poems from so many amazing writers. Equally, it has been an honor to connect with every single one of our readers. This journey has meandered from New Zealand to South Africa to Poland to Taiwan to Serbia to Cornwall and Wales, with so many other stops along the way.

This spring we find ourselves immersed in Slovakia. Guest editor and translator Nina Varon and I connected through some Serbian writer-friends. Poets seem always to find one another. Never be shy about approaching one—just be prepared to talk for a while. Slovakian history is a tale of resilience and reconstruction and reclamation—and this poetry is enlightening and inspiring. Varon worries that too few people are willing to listen to Slovakian poets, and so we are pleased to amplify their voices.

It is impossible for me not to find myself in this collection of poems. It would seem that the person I was and the person I have become is being reflected back to me. The first poem, "How Is She," begins with a series of questions:

> How is the poem before she gets written?
> Is she young, naïve, does she want to know more,
> Will she not wait by my pen to be bitten,
> Or will she weave herself into my score?

Yes, that is what the beginning was like for me. The final poem, "Enclosure," is exactly where I find myself now: "in spaces in buildings in cultures…I am thinking about how to get out." This is an encapsulation of my time as editor.

When I published the first of my editor's notes, I said: "I have accepted the position knowing that I will never accomplish what Dan has—building a world-class journal from nothing." I leave my post proud to have (forgive my mixing of metaphors) steered this ship through some difficult waters—bringing her safely to shore in her new home. Throughout this journey, JC Reilly has worked beside me. You may not have noticed that she quietly slipped into the role of co-editor in the last issue. I can never fully express to her my gratitude.

Apologies for so much self-indulgence, but it difficult to say good-bye—even when you know that the time has come. As Ace Boggess offers in his poem "Moving Furniture," "This is transition & conclusion / until the future tells us Start again." Meanwhile, know that *Atlanta Review* will always occupy the most special of places in my heart, but, more importantly, I look forward to the brightest of futures for the journal at it remarkably enters its third decade of publication.

Sending you all much love,

Karen

Wanting More, or On Having a Baby at 42

The baby smashes giant black ant-like berries into her mouth,
one by one. The juice trails; segments cling to her cheek, chin,
and somehow, forehead. Especially slippery berries are sent rolling
across the floor, destined for a delayed squish between unknowing adult
           toes.
And then! a sound previously unknown—one syllable made multiple
and the pitch a frequency falling so far off the right of any known scale.
With the context clue of the empty plastic mini-bowl, somehow
you make out the word, "MORE," from the multilayers of squeak and
           squeal
gushing from tiny lips. You and your husband share a look,
automatically mimic the word, first to each other and then to the child.
A mistake—the baby, witnessing the delight—and appreciating
the immediacy with which her bowl is refilled—claims the word
as one of her own six (now seven), destined for repeat.
How many more years will you get to feed her glee?
This is how deals with the devil get done.

Erin Aube

Peacocks Will Have the Last Word*

I walk at Andalusia with Mama and Charlotte
in May, when it's not-yet summer, but trace sweat on my lips.
In Georgia, I'll never know what spring tastes like.

We stroll the grounds, and Flannery's house
is its own small paradise today. No other visitors
crowd us. The museum's volunteers back inside leave us be.

I wonder if Heaven's like the place I've always called home;
bursting oaks, with limbs like arms—Adam reaching for God,
daughter for mother, friend for friend, self for soul—
chords of cicadas that pierce the nightly honey-dipped haze,
yellow sun that digs beneath the skin, it's in the marrow.

Will Mama be there? Will Charlotte? Will I?

At Andalusia, the peacocks hypnotize us. Astor, the male,
teases us with his tail, a celestial blue I cannot memorize.

I'm about to graduate. I'm about to move away, and
I wonder if I'll come back here. As if reading my mind,
Mama fills the silence with stories—our first trip to Flannery's,

when I never thought I'd live in Milledgeville, and
I guess Flannery didn't think she would either.

By my age, Flannery had already lived over half her life.
By my age, Mama had been nine years a wife.
I know only the oaks, the cicadas, the sun.

Flannery kept forty peacocks at a time. Have I ever loved
anything as much as Flannery loved her birds?

I want answers. Astor watches me,
and I almost believe he recognizes me—
one wandering soul acknowledging another.

He steps toward me, eyes glint with promise,
as if to show me a glimpse of Heaven,

and in an instant, his feathers close.

Brittany J. Barron

Note:
The poem title is inspired by Flannery O'Connor's concluding statement in her essay
"Living with a Peacock" (1961).

Hitchhiking I Met an Actor Who Appeared on TV with Lassie #17

Handsome at 6'4 Don looked like a young Rock Hudson and he loved to
suck long Cuban cigars... He showed me how to play excellent croquet
standing close behind me with his arms around me—his steady hands
guiding mine on the smooth hard stiff mallet's handle. I was good,
but he easily won early games with better aim and best ball speed.

An actor, he also did stand-up comedy in nightclubs in Hollywood.
I read a framed newspaper clipping he'd saved about his appearance
on the Lassie TV show, with a yellowing photo of him a "a local
hometown hero shaking Lassie #17's famous paw!" Later we enjoyed
spaghetti, red wine and French bread for a delicious meal together.

That night in his A-frame he copied Johnny Carson's best jokes in a
three-ring binder and told me some funny L.A. gossip of his own...
He said I could share his only bed or flop on a firm fold-down sofa.
I was tired of sleeping in boxcars, laundromats, churches and barns.
So I gladly took his friendly offer. Barely into my first dry dream

his warm hand stroked my young thigh as I knew it would. It felt
okay, but I declined. He yawned, "That's fine. I never force myself
on anyone." At breakfast I watched him lick yellow yolks over easy
from the sharp tines of his long fork... Later his old white-haired
father arrived—frowning at me as he delivered a wrapped package...

The father looked like Alexander Calder eyeing me suspiciously under
two balanced bushy white eyebrows. Later, Don and I swam nude in a
cool green quarry-pond following his ninth straight croquet victory.
We sunned our wet bodies like lazy lizards on flat limestone hunks
scattered across a grassy landscape like ruins of an ancient temple.

Don drove me to Boston the next day so he could "shop for sailors..."
I met a nice guy there at the Y who let me flop on his floor free.
He flipped hamburgers in a diner and smuggled some home for me. His
penny-loafers curled up at their toes like used elf slippers. Lonely,
divorced, missing his kids, we knew free hamburgers were temporary.

R. Steve Benson

Moving Furniture

Around tight corners, down narrow stairs.
Elbows bump doorknobs.
Knees buckle. Back petitions
for redress of grievances.

This could be living
or the tiresome, painful path toward death.
Or is it truth on Saturday
reordering the staccato world?

The futon must go to the curb.
Mattress, also. Save the box springs,
put-together frame. Too many chairs—
choices must be made.

This is the first farewell between
lovers parting briefly in the rain.
This is transition & conclusion,
until the future tells us *Start again*.

Ace Boggess

The Vibration of Water

Say what you will but I believe water
speaks to water: glacier to cirrus,
fog to aquifer. An amniotic sac
breaks and groundwater quivers.
I turn on my tap and fill my glass,
water mixed with tree run off and tears
from Aleppo. I drink, and my lungs,

mostly water, feels somehow
some other mother's shuddering breath.
I believed my son was safe in Syria
in those early years, that karma could shelter
him and all the other aid workers.
I wouldn't hear from him for weeks
but I'd stand at night in the rain

under the towering cedars and firs
of the Pacific Northwest and feel him
on my face as I beseeched the clouds.
Something like a black locomotive
made of rainclouds filled my dreams
and I wept with relief. All that water.
He would come home, and I knew it.

I felt it hum in the fathom of my bones.

Michele Bombardier

Ugly Fruit

Last night I drove around
behind the grocery store
as I make a point to do.
There are things to be found there
like racks of cinnamon bread,
still wrapped, just a little mold,
bananas just a little brown.
This time I spot a grocery cart
with sagging pumpkins,
jostled one on the other
like kids crowded
onto a rickety carnival ride.

I know how proud
pumpkins can look,
lined up on their seasonal stands,
promising pies,
aspiring to be jack-o-lanterns.
And then there were these guys.
At first I dismissed them,
but then I kept thinking
how bad could they be?
It takes so little
to be tossed out these days.

I thought of those pumpkins
as I walked my dog
and imagined one roasting,
my little home filled with the scent
of pumpkin muffins, pumpkin soup.
I returned and sure enough,
beneath the rot
there was a white one
with just a spot on its bottom.
I carried it back, composted the pulp,
set the seeds aside for toasting,
brushed the halves with oil,

garden rosemary, coarse salt
and I roasted its unspoiled flesh,
yellow and forgiving.

Grey Brown

Lubbock Storms

With the cotton harvested and packed
into roadside monoliths, hollowed soil cries
of hunger. Always a good listener, the sky

remembers its duty to spill and whips up
an east wind bringing clouds of sand.
Red dust makes a sunset you can touch

and fills your molars with grit.
The storm's cough grates against buildings
as pigeons tuck themselves into terracotta cubbies

in the library's walls. Courtyard grackles
fall silent for the first and last time as I stare
into the storm: heavy, gluttonous, dried-blood black.

At last, the faint sun glows like a pin-prick
through tarp, and over the dust stripping
car paint comes a grackle's single, throaty cry.

William Brown

Lyrics

Being a trumpet player, my lips sealed
in brass, I never learned the lyrics. Yes,
I know the great jazz voices—Ella, Etta,
phlegmy Satchmo—who sing like angels.
Not me. Dumb as my dog when it comes
to the words, in fact any language seems
inadequate...

      Compare the spoken word love
to a horn player's muted solo, touching
the pit of primal memory, a misty whisper
before there were nouns, escaping
reason, logic, thought. Truth is
I can't remember what I didn't learn,
instead tune to keys or scat or made-up
verse. I hope you'll forgive me
when I try to sing of love.

Peter Neil Carroll

Wetlands

I am writing this underwater, to be clear, a mangle
of wetlands, a tangle of marsh at the foot of the hill where
my father built our home on the Rappahannock River

in Virginia, because wetlands were cheap, and he
loved to fish. And crab. It's not hard to write underwater
when you spend all day crabbing. I recall baiting traps, trapping

crabs, tripping over gills and claws shaken from trap onto dock,
slipping on crab slime, how my summer was one slip-up after
another, was the hoisting of our haul, was my father and his steel

pot bubbling, blue crabs boiling blue, was me in hot water, throwing
crabs back in the creek, crabs skittering to freedom, their sideways
flight so etched in my mind that I saw it when I went off the college

in Connecticut where it was too blue cold for blue crabs. I saw it.
The splintered dock. The rusted traps. The slimed rope. My father.
The barnacles. The stars. My father would spin us under the night sky,

quiz us—"Where is Cancer?"—each constellation his catch. "There is
Pisces," he boomed. At dinner, my father would say a grace that
began "Lord, thank you for this meal," which meant this catch,

our catch, bless our catch of the day, catch me if you can—my father
praying with his bait-your-hook-now voice, "There is a girl here
which hath five barley loaves and two fishes, and the two fishes

she divided among all and they all did eat—all five thousand," my
father praying, his prayer catching on the wooden mallet
that cracked open the claws, crabs crushed, hot pot boiling

over, how the water sustained us, and how we crouched low
in the lightening, under cracks of thunder, how we hoisted the traps,
and when I think of home—I think of our backyard sinking, the soil

reeking, fish heads floating, my tee shirt molding, how the jellyfish
stings on my arm burned and itched like crazy, my father sprinkling
Adolf's meat tenderizer on my arms, singing. "We are anglers, Annie,
     anglers,"

Adolf's flying in my eyes, a cigar in his other hand, my hair
stiff with salt water, summers so long, winters lonely, sun
like thunder, dock like train tracks, the creek running fast to the Bay.

Ann Chinnis

Emily Brontë in Manhattan

A woman's pelisse—furry, like wild cotton-grass
in the Haworth moorlands—brushed my arm.
> This textured city
screeches, calling attention to everything at once.
Crowds guide me to the tunnel where trains race
toward a terminal with constellations painted on the ceiling.
> I mind the echoes.

A bouquet of purple heather lures me. The chief distraction
has been a round man sausageing from café to café,
> neck glistening sweat.
Though frightening as an increase in taxes,
the city's grey towers reach incredible heights.
I pause inside a large, stretched shadow
> to enjoy its coolness.

The orange-bellied birds (may I call them robins?)
belong to a series of alleys. Matrices of streets
> tease me with
suspended boxes blinking colorful lights.
The soles of my feet take over the conversation.
The clouds here are half the terror of Yorkshire's;
> I'd pay for some rain.

In the air, a meaty smell overwhelms a baby's wail.
I discover an oasis of greenery. At the park's edge:
> a triumphant arch.
I settle on a wooden bench and peek
into the window of a shop with a pink door:
a case full of cakes, pastries, biscuits . . .
> how sweet would the frosting taste?

Chloe Cook

A Yard Full of Promises

The spade goes into the soil with a "clunk." It's a stone, I hope
and I say it out loud because I want my daughter to think that, too.
There is no room for morbid speculation
about bodies buried in the garden, a box full of the previous owner's dead
      cat
when you're the adult in charge. "Yep, it's a stone," I say again
as I carefully push my fingers around the object,
smooth, round, a pit for an eye socket. No, it's a stone.

Next to me, my daughter rambles on excitedly about buried treasure
the possibility of some other child's old toys hiding beneath the soil
all sorts of magical things. I bury myself in her speculations, fill my own
      head
with thoughts of secret portals and tiny doorways,
magical tunnels that lead to fairy kingdoms
blocked off from the real world by a large, round,
skull-shaped rock.

Holly Day

Rings of Moon Light

In the park, I once heard
a bullfrog croak

and above the dark trees
the moon peered down

at me between branches
like a face in a window

looking at my little domestic
scene, one that includes

its rippling face in the pond
that I am so fond of

where the frog spoke
and broke the water's tension.

Deborah H. Doolittle

We Thirst

We are thirsty for mercy.
Three times today a hummingbird
came to my face.
Searching my eyes.

The buzz more poignant than
any lovers I've taken.
Fearful at first by a sting that
comes with a buzz.

Feed me feed me says the spinning jewel.
There is a needy god in that click
that flit of effervescent.
I fall into the need to quench.

We are thirsty for love.
Two times yesterday hummingbirds
came to my lips.
These lips that also whisper hunger.

So close I felt desire sizzling
my unfolding passion wanting
to open like the hibiscus so
they could drink. Opening my mouth
to your mouth. Breathe life into me.

J.V. Foerster

Psamtik to Psammetichus

(after Herodotus 2.2.2)

The language of air is lightning—when it speaks
the heavens split in a tongue as old as sound.
The house communicates in sighs and creaks.
The language of the lightning is called thunder.
Two bodies speak in a language known as love.
The mountain speaks by murmuring from the ground,
or screams, in wind and flames and death. I wonder—
if language is a language, then what of?
The ash is the expression of the spark.
Bodies speak to bodies using violence.
The language of the dog is bite, not bark.
The voice of air is written in flights of birds.
There is a Language of Truth—it's simply silence,
and the Language of Lies, which translates all, is words.

Daniel Galef

Note:
According to Herodotus, the pharaoh Psamtik attempted to discover the primordial
and inherent language of humanity by having a pair of children raised without ever
being taught or spoken to.

Nocturne 60

Sheer night, night's sheen—
faint curtain of starlight

              between

    I and nothing,
    nothing and nothing,
    I and the nevertheless of I.
*

Frayed ends woven to patterns
    ending and/or beginning
    in an overhead array
    of spark and/or smolder.

            I

between the nothing of
and the nothing but

           me,

beneath the stars as between the stars
that gently rest in downy bedding
    of before the beginning
    and after the end.
*

The tactile of the lightness of such lights,
of the lightliness of my striding through
    as striding by.

Jeff Graham

Gillying

We spend Whitsun with family friends in Wells.
On a grey, salt and slate morning, we set up
on the quay with plastic buckets and fishing lines
that unravel like kite strings. Our legs dangle
over the stone dock whilst mothers attach raw bacon,
the colour of bad wine, to blunted hooks.

We lean carefully, balanced on the edge
of something, lower bait into the green water.
The murk below begins to move: a congregation
of crabs gather around our bounty,
believing it offered by a benevolent God.
They do not seem to know this has happened before;
they clamber and grab with the claws of the starving.

Our lines are plucked like harp strings as we make
the first haul. A crab is lifted towards the light,
crashes through the surface, dripping seaweed
from wriggling legs. Its black shell glitters
in the strengthening sun. This is rapture.
Crabs mass against the harbour wall,
desperate to be one of the chosen.

An hour passes and our buckets, monoliths,
miniature aquariums, become loud with
a crustacean clatter. The saltwater is congealed
with struggling bodies, dark and heavy as blood.
Our parents grow restless, groaning for fish and chips.

After a hasty count, a winner is declared,
and we scramble to our feet, tip the buckets.
A tide of crabs, clacking at their salvation,
is washed back to the depths; they drop
like stones to the seafloor. We see an exchange
of peace with the waiting, and imagine
they are sharing their glimpse of heaven.

Bex Hainsworth

Pandora

Don't
    believe
        for
            one
                second
that I didn't know what I was
doing. I opened that darn box,
felt the weight of wrath, ran a
finger down the cool metal of
ruthlessness, and gave women
the tools for their revenge.

Bex Hainsworth

breaking: Roe

this is what the subject line read, and I know it's right, the concept
or how to conceive as a woman now owned by a man and here,
supreme court, hold my uterus. if it's such a fragile thing, so precious
to you, if every red blood cell that has fallen through it is a gift from
god, if every used pad, every child I did not have because I lost three
pregnancies is somehow sacred to you, then I should be a saint in
your eyes. every woman risen in the cloud of *holy-god-almighty-see-
how-white-he-is*, see our menstrual blood born red as the martyrs
but transformed in law to the purity of a lamb, if my scream of back
labor was a heavenly cry worthy of archangels in flight, if my epi-
dural sliced into my spine the wrong way has truly left me with the
holy relic of arthritis in each boxed vertebra, if almost watching my
one child be stillborn, and another miscarried, if waiting for a doctor
to ask permission to save my life, if the birth of my youngest created
in her lungs a stammer in harmonic time, to sing with the cherubim,
if my life and my daughters' lives, they who carry the eggs they were
born with, are so very alabaster and carved righteous as a stunning
virgin from the very first day they opened their eyes, is my son no
more or less holy, is my son born to be the christ of me, his mother
mary, born to descend from a cross because it is the descent that
matters most, condescending to pay for my sins, the sins of my body
and never my ovum, and this is what I don't understand as I read the
ruling declaring my uterus, my ovaries and theirs, my fallopian tubes
so easily blocked, my surgery scars and endometrial hyperplasia, my
grief pain scream loss as only an altar, waiting for a lifetime of
sacrifice: if I am born so loved, when did the hate begin?

Mare Heron Hake

Compassion

like the snow that falls
last on the ground in the thickest forest
because it takes so long to make

its way down through the pine boughs
and branches but falls all at once on
the roofs and yards, train tracks

fields and meadows roads and sidewalks
frozen lakes, paths and riverbanks
on people's hats, bare heads and hands

some winters the piles so high
no one bothers to put their shovels
away until spring, other years

there are vast distances to cross
under cloudy skies that refuse
to soften shine or give

Joanne Holdridge

Losing His Light

Hard long sad slow hurting day
up and out of the house before dawn
to drive northeast before the traffic
I got stuck in anyway, going and returning
to see a friend whose cancer is back
round 2 arriving at the start of plague
chemo, radiation, stem cell transplant
blood transfusions, the usual miasma
of what's worse the sickness or its maybe

cure, even vaccinated and boostered
isolating and testing before I go
I wear an N-95 mask, stay at a distance
hands washed and sanitized, wanting to
be close, but too afraid to touch
forget about hold his hand or stroke
his hair, instead we sit and talk
until he tires and then his wife
and I go for a long walk out

in the blustery cold down the narrow
spit of land where the road ends
and the harbor at Ten Pound Island
gives way to open sea
the waves rough and gray
rocks white with icy sleet and spray
I imagine the wind blasting
plague out to sea, blowing in fresh
cold salty air healing my friend

who is too weak to stand
and I know with all that's in me
to know but wishes something else
that he's dying, just before I leave
I touch my fingers to the cold windowpane

and on the other side of that freezing pane
he pulls out from somewhere intentional
the ghost of his old grin

Joanne Holdridge

Down Payment

Dad left me enough for the down payment
and that was sufficient   I don't blame
him for not having more to parcel out

between us brothers   he spent his life
welding railroad track   retiring early
before his body broke apart

before cancer infiltrated his guts
he took me fishing when I was young
but I was an ungrateful wretch

pissing and moaning about the cold and dirt
and the worms that gave me the creeps
and the fish that we never caught

unable then to comprehend that merely
being together was all he wanted and needed
I remember his Brylcreem   and the Vicks VapoRub

the way he smelled when he came home from work
the dirt engrained in the skin of his hands
and the fumes that permeated his work shirts

my brother sold the house and split the proceeds
we'll probably never go to that town again
never drink in the pub where dad sat with me

nursing his pint   until my brothers were
old enough to take his place   after which
he stayed home and slowly grew old

as the river gradually deepened its cleft
in the stone beneath the viaduct   and the crows
flitted from tree to tree   preparing us for winter.

Paul Ilechko

Zeroes and Ones

The records show I've loved you
since the birth of my databases.
Files declare I've known you

since heaven sent me down here
to find your embrace, to promise
you I won't let you go. Folders

full of rough drafts of my affection,
completed missives from my heart,
are yours to delete or save to another

computer, one shaped like your heart.
My system runs on images of you,
eating an ice cream cone, taking out

trash. Every minor task you perform
lets me access the only feelings I have.
Your recorded voice, those MP3s,

are songs I play in my ear before I sleep,
so I can recall each pitch and timbre.
When my memory collapses, the end

of my machine, I'll try to remember
that we loved once, zeroes and ones,
in an order no one could take away.

Donald Illich

All Around Us Would Be Spring

For Rachel, May 2020

In another version of this time
you would let me hold your baby.

She would be curled, curled upon my breast as we walked
side-by-side and tumbling toward the water.

There would still be wild daisies doubled overhead
and a sea of grass turning gold beneath the green.

With your child in my arms, I'd feel like we were sisters
—as I did sometimes when we were children.

I'd know for sure then, that some things come back blooming
even after they've been fallow.

Tess K. Jacobs

Reparation Montage

"Have you ever dreamed it was all given back?"
–Jacob Meders

I dream the hummingbirds tripled once
Japanese honeysuckle untethered from the earth.

And we found all the frogs that disappeared in the nineties
blooming from under leaves, eyes gleaming like the sheen

of black tulip petals. The oaks released their fingers
from the throat of the underbrush. When people say

for every 100 that are reported there are 10,000 you don't see,
this time they mean frogs and not women.

My grandmother walks alone when the sun goes down,
that she naps as much as she prays—constantly, that the rosary isn't

a meal replacement, and she cooks *sos pwa* for both of us.
Mothers sleep with their daughters in another room

and not beneath their legs. And worship
is not a place but a rhythm, voice raised

in hymns and beating feet. And we greet
each other with a hand shake or finger snap,

don't kiss each other at all when we leave
the house—we know we'll see each other again.

Siobhan Jean-Charles

Clouds Rise

in the north like templed shrouds
above the prairie, shadows
like the ghosts of snow.

Cold as memory, this road back
holy in its lack
of sentiment. The crow

awaits in nearby bracken.
Sunlight hurts the eyes,
a comfort only to the wise.

P M F Johnson

chronometria

time passes through body,

a fact which I challenge with a walk
at an equal and opposite rate
in the obverse direction,

beneath a sky that's been bruised,
by the splitting sun,
which somehow still paints
the city beautiful,

rosying the still cheeks of buildings
over which a cool wind skims,
stenting open the flue in my chest,
and grazing the crease that was carved

in my lips with a kiss long ago,
from the same one whose
fingerprints ripened into freckles
down my spine.

most things last longer than people,
except for the body,
which sheds huge drifts of nails and skin,
and makes a snowglobe of my vacuum,

and an abacus for the kernels of time.

Sophie Liebergall

The Water Garden

that summer there was no girl left in me—
so i cracked the wings of twenty butterflies, smearing my eyelids with
            neoprene blues

and i know you thought i was crazier than you…

when I met you here I see you first
beyond dimension shining forth
as we carried so many glistening rain coats
clapping endless, right into the night

what is it about falling that makes everything seem so bright?

(Hear that?)
            (No.)

and now, and now, and now…

            (Listen…)

somewhere, *here*,
a new country is arriving…

the rain in trastevere is always a sound at first
when small specks of black ash fall so slow all around us

i reach out to grasp something we can hold here, together
before the world slips through our open hands like water

i uncurl my fingers
and catch a faint black mark there…

flocks of a million starlings gather each day in rome as
though it were some strange natural phenomena caused by
unseen forces though we cannot see or explain why this
occurs. I search for the reason continuously

Jessica Lim

Bedtime Prayer on Behest

Matt tells me, after I beg yet again,
I already told you my answer.
My body makes the shape of silent
pleading. He knows I want to hear
his answer on repeat, the way our
someday maybe child might want
to hear the same bedtime story told
every night for a year like a prayer.
His voice has the same fond softness
for me as the sweatpants I've stolen
from his next-door drawer. He speaks
into me, *I would be content even*
without a child. I will be happy
as long as I'm with you. His eyes,
a sleeping mask for my insomniac
soul. His arms, my favorite comforter
especially when the weather inside
my unmothered mind goes cold.

Jenny Maaketo

Distal

It snowed last night in the south hills. Yet
a friend has already planted her peas
and the daphne's blooming under my window.

It snowed last night in the south hills, but
we've started planning road trips again.
Unfolding maps, imagining itineraries.

We think we're far from the action here,
safely distanced from the warzones. We can read
and watch history happening through a spyglass.

Ripples reach us diminished by the vast expanse
of continents. And we're okay
not being any closer.

Focused on the little local, tending our peas,
we're liable to forget how close the fires
that fall, that winter, that whole long year.

Ash drifting from the sky.
Windows sealed tight.

Karen McPherson

My First Orchid

Peach, fuchsia-colored sexes at their centers.
   When one bloom begins to dry, indicated
by a line of brown along the edges, I think
   that I am fine. I haven't killed my first orchid,
flower my daddy has babied since before
   he fathered me. His veins parallel, like theirs.
And since my blood is half his, I must
   have some orchid in me, too. So I water
with his care, soak & drain, cup the pot's
   surface so the chips don't litter the sink.
I refuse to let oily fingers touch tendril
   roots, eye those that slither & burrow
like snakes around pot's circumference,
   and I want to be them, for absorption to be
synonymous with breathing. When I check
   the plant again, the bloom has fallen, I let
its stem rest between pointer & middle, using
   fingertips to flick at once-thick petals, now
feathery. Others are starting to go, more faces
   beginning to cave into themselves, so I phone
my daddy, tell him how the blooms dry & fall
   and he says, among other things, he thinks
my first orchid is not getting enough sun.

Arianna Miller

The Way Home

Days grow shorter, but the heat still blisters. I long to flee
from my own left bloodied eye and its blurred plans.

Today by the pool's jagged edge a great egret. I glimpse
his black beak, his green eye and white feathers before he collapses

into the blue. At two beats per-second he'll be at Bolsa Chica wetlands
in an hour. The escaped African song bird birders call a *parasite* is still here.

Like last year a solo, distinct in his small body and long tail. He tries to fit
in, but the finches chase him away. Don't we all try to fit in? The neighbor,

his unleashed dog, Lola, his base that beats on and on. His voice rises,
Come home, momma when he calls his dog. We wonder away.

Sometimes we adopt a new home like when I was the only single mom
on Snowden Avenue. I stopped for a beer with a neighbor on his front lawn.

I tried to fit in, even if I didn't like the taste of Coors. On this scorched day
the female whydah lays her eggs in the garden finch's nest. She abandons

them and joins the ground pigeons. She is still trying to fit in. A poet I know
and I once exchanged thoughts on home. I remember him saying,

Where is home actually? When I consider what home means I recall back
to when my father held on so tight. He lay in his hospital bed riddled

with cancer and filled with morphine. I think back about to what he wanted
when he gripped my hand in his calloused hand and whispered the word,
    home.

If only, I could have had the strength of the egret to lift into the February sky
on that dark day. If only, I could have carried his frail body home.

Florence Murry

After Long Illness

You called me to the window. And I rose
from bed and saw the two fawns

that had drifted into the yard. Dew clung
on the grass. One of the fawns stooped

to crop the white morning glories
stitched like initials in the green fabric.

And the flowers, without complaint or grief,
yielded themselves to the nibbling teeth,

only to reappear on the soft brown pelt,
like sunlight dappled on the forest floor.

Derek N. Otsuji

Squall

Grey gulls in blown snow mar the absolute,
scoring staggered arcs on the wet sky,
iambic stroke of wings impaired by struggle
to hold a course against the beating gusts.
One dips to skim a shimmer from the water
with mortal precision, despite wind-shear, a glide
and spearing thrust, and the inchling fish is there,
then not, a flick of the head to swallow, and wings
work hard to climb again, as any mind
labours behind events, where description is
an account of the past, even the mind's story
about itself. This is not a simple page
of birds and weather, though the lake throws cold
at me, wind shaves curls of foam from break-
ers' crests. I need the words for this and think:
this icy winter hisses, this killing winter coos
and coddles; it dawdles and strokes my brow,
my hands, my neck, my poor measure of warmth
inviting the lewd hunger of circling gulls.

James Owens

Heirlooms

Grandma six weeks dead and not a thing
left to me—her diamond ring, her pearls
distributed among my mother and sisters.

Last week, I watched a neighbor in the yard,
untangling her tomato vines
like king snakes from the wire into a trellis.
Yellow blossoms punctuated each leaf.

I almost asked the neighbor
for some tomato seeds, just enough
to grow my own—two or three,
maybe some basil or mint too—
which Scott thinks is ridiculous,
there's not a green thumb between us.

I'm no good at pretending the earth isn't dying
with each wringing out of the clouds.

Once more, Scott and I try to revive
the parlor palm from his father's funeral.
The roots have gone to shit,
the leaves like shriveled snakeskins.

Christian, grandma would say
as my sisters and I played under her tangerine tree,
One day, I will watch your children.
Just to say I tried,

I dig myself deeper
and deeper into the earth.

Christian Paulisich

Fragments of History

An entire people carried theirs
across a desert. Etched it in tombs.
On Sundays, I heard parables
of fire & water, whales gulping
people whole. Now, I read them
to my children. Perspective settled
on me like a new wool sweater.
All stories are ours. In sixth grade,
my teacher swore he was haunted
by the ghost of a miner. He would
wake up at night to a man slumped
on the foot of his bed, or heaving
a wheelbarrow back-&-forth. *Ghosts
are a type of history, too*, he said.
Wind is the history of the atmosphere.
Light, the history of the sun. A tree
stump is the history of a flashing hatchet,
but also the history of a tree. The road is
a history of tires & wandering feet. I want
my history to be told the way the moon
gushes of the sun, devoted, glowing
at the thought of it. Ancient astronomers
made maps of the sky—space-ferried
histories of stars—from light years
away. So historical are we, scriptural,
that even our bones are stowed like
old letters. & when I die, I imagine
mine will lie like a moon in the darkness
—as precise as precise can be—
all so someone behind the rot of time
can peel back the lid from a pine box & say:
My, my, my. Hello, Gorgeous. Who were we?

Seth Peterson

The Circus

Georges Seurat, 1891

Hundreds of tiny dots,
blue and yellow, converge
on an alien green ballerina,
balanced on one toe atop
a pale horse circling the ring.

She is about to be flung
sideways into space, a slanted
accident before wide-eyed
spectators ready to applaud
her imminent demise but
distracted by the acrobat
walking on his hands.

In the foreground, a white-faced
jester grins, bells jingling
on a three-pointed red cap,
and to his right, a black-suited
ringmaster pulls back the curtain
on the scene. The audience

wonders what it would be like
to fly through the air in a tutu,
arms akimbo, not knowing
where to land. Or to exist in the flesh
of a raucous clown, or an impresario
who makes of life a show.

Seurat juggled dots on a canvas,
settling them into patterns of old ochre.
He carefully planned his palette,
more important than the death
of a dancer, the jokes of a jester,
the balance of an upside-down
acrobat. The painting, it's said,

remains unfinished, the spun gold
of the big-top circus still spinning
somewhere in the yellowish ether.

Donna Pucciani

Daphne,

I dreamt your roots retracted from the earth
When I returned the shoots I'd pruned to make a wreath.

The branches intertwined and took the shape of limbs;
The bark turned skin, the kind of white behind blood swims.

And metamorphosis continued as your leaves
Went autumn brown in bliss, no rustling, now at ease,

Content to hang in quiet strands that spilled to trace
The soft emerging limit of your placid face.

Soon every feature you had shed from memory
Renewed, though fixed into a silent treasury,

Until your lips were broken, drawing air so deep;
At once your eyes flung open—startling me from sleep.

*

My eyes timed with the sun, and in the brightness searched
For laurels that were gone. No doubt that they were perched

On someone else's head, since years had passed from when
I'd paid them mind. Instead, to counterfeiting men

They traded every day, a trophy bought and sold,
As none of them could say that anything would hold.

Daphne, what can I give but promise? I'll undo
The wrong and you will live. The wreath I took from you

I'll win to end this curse that kept you from my hands.
And let it be in verse, I have no more demands.

I'd rather see your face roam free where I can't follow
Than trapped within one place. Forever yours,

Apollo

Justin Pulice

Luck Will Still Smile on Us

—line from the Ukrainian national anthem

My husband says, *You can always find something
to be sad about.* I tell him, my people were born
like this, with hearts that murmur. Flutter.

Beat too much. Our hearts have singed edges.
They rain cold soot on the streets of Kyiv.
They regurgitate the crusted blood of soldiers

who lie wounded in a filthy ward of cots,
and in walks Zelensky, to hand a medal
to each one. Zelensky, murmuring thanks,

leans down to a soldier, in his weary bed,
and whispers in his ear....
                             Wouldn't it be great if he started,

"A minister, priest, and a rabbi walk into a bar...."

After all, our hearts will kick-start with a joke.
After all, he's a comic, one of us, but with biceps
and steadier heart.

How does the world goes on?
Murmur and flutter:

the doves are still arriving
in Independence Square, and the soldiers

stationed with Kalashnikovs are tearing bits
of rationed bread that fall to the pavement.

A woman hands out blue and yellow tulips.
And outside the opera house a choir stands

lacquered in sun
and birds fly out of each mouth

Kathy Shorr

Zinnias Grow in My Adult Garden

I didn't plant them here in the shady corner of my backyard,
the only flowers left behind by the couple who sold me this house.

It's late summer and they're tired of suntracking.
Spindly stems lie across pavers like necks in a guillotine.

Heads rest outside the flower bed, petals paused mid explosion.
Petals as spokes lodged in my throat: I haven't seen

such fireworks since Dad planted every pink,
yellow, orange in my childhood. I colored fiercely

with those crayons, yet to see them within reach
after so much time—bright and blunt—I am Pinocchio

got no strings to hold me down, save the phantom
tug of Geppetto. It's wrong to plant zinnias in shade,

but how dare memory be the one to ask: Why reach
for the sun just to become a myriad broken tipped knives?

I am a child entering a garden past its prime,
the dirt-stained knees of his denim just behind the curtain.

Grief's dull edge: petals as grace notes.
I too want to lie down, exhausted from reaching for sun.

Caroline Simpson

Why My Father Insists on Arriving Early at Ben Gurion Airport

The first time through security,
a soldier thumbs my father's
American passport, stops
at his birthplace, Aleppo.
Suitcases removed from X-ray,
outstretched arms order us
to the back of the line.

The second time, a soldier motions
for a group of men wearing yarmulkes
to walk in front of us. We don't belong.
A soldier asks my sister if she
is my father's wife. When she says,
"he's my father," he responds, "right,
your husband."

The third time our suitcases roll
toward the X-ray, now giddy
as the machine swallows
my Samsonite, I start to approach
the metal detector until an arm
cradling a machine gun points us
to the end of the line, again.

Jen Siraganian

Widow Fog

Houses huddle closely, shiver as the street
forms a tunnel under the low, dark sky.
The slowing down season begins. Cold creeps
into bones, my heart now a dead end shut

by sorrow. Trees have dropped their camouflage.
Naked branches rise, pure form in this false
death. The ground digs into itself, takes on
a husk, drab with faded grays, blacks, and browns.

Underneath small creatures keep earth alive,
moving below the frozen shell. Having
banked fires of desire, whenever
I wake and face into cold air I feel

sharpness in my marrow, become quickly
alert, bow my head, mourn Norman's passing,
and hope soon to depart winter mind,
spring with life into warm flowering sun.

Marilynn Tallal

LBJ in the Rotunda

A long line of people in the cold black night
And we were there, my father, twenty-year-old sister,
And me, not quite ten, in my black coat. Earlier that school year
Our fourth-grade teacher had asked
The name of the only living ex-president
And I, alone and proud, knew.
I didn't know much more.
Little about the Civil Rights Act, less about Vietnam,
The angel and devil on the shoulders
Of this gray-haired foul-mouthed living ex-president, now dead.
What I mainly understood, as I stood under the black sky,
Waiting to view not the man himself but
His flag-draped coffin,
Was that I was cold—and happy that
My sister kept calling me a "trooper,"
For being so young and waiting so cold, a Black boy
Poised between pain and pride.

Clifford Thompson

Before You Leave

You will be asked to thread the sun
with a purple arrow as a needle,
pulling a silver-stranded tail.
When it spirals through and falls back
into gravity, you must catch it and tie it up.

You will be asked to attach to its top rim
a horizontal black shade to block
its light, to allow night its covered
respite.

Then you will be asked to love and forgive
in whatever order possible,
and to walk and talk and eat with loss
after it ties your feet and tapes your mouth.
And when it frees you, you must provide it
with a room in your house forever.

Marie Gray Wise

Of Poetry and Mourning

all the lovely poems
begin in nature: with streams
or orchids, turtles,
or deer—

delicious sensual descriptions
lead us to or are themselves metaphors
that take us somewhere else—
from ice to joy, or more likely,
from joy to immutable reality
and the pretense that it can be
cushioned by the poignancy
of pristine details

you and I did not have much traffic
with nature beyond planting flowers
or that early trip to Mount Shasta
where you fished and I lit the small hibachi grill

after that we traded the sleek yellow Kharmann Ghia
for a sturdy beige Volkswagen station wagon
planning to camp, though we never did—
that early yearning part of the nesting process
a return to basics: man, woman, fire

and so, love, I have no spiderwebs
or petals or anything delicate
to wend my way to mourning
all I have is plain flat sorrow
and still, two clenched hands

Marie Gray Wise

International Feature Section

Slovakia

Edited by

Nina Varon & Miriam Margala

Translated by

Nina Varon

Introduction to Slovak Poetry

Coming from the central European region, the uniqueness of Slovak poetry remains undiscovered. It offers such richness of poetic voices, that it is difficult to categorize the contemporary authors in any way, all of them worlds unto themselves. Readers in Slovakia are fortunate to have many beautifully bound and illustrated collections at their fingertips to choose from. Whether they prefer traditional lyricism or modern experimental texts, they can be sure to read high quality poetry. In recent years, the popularity of poetry, and its readership, has been growing—a welcoming development.

The history of Slovak poetry includes a normative period, which was not conducive to originality and creativity. Poems published in the communist times of the post-war Czechoslovakia (mid-20th century) were highly stylized, celebrating the heroism of the proletariat. Any poetry that deviated from the communist ideals could not be published; with the exception of the 1960s "thaw" in the regime when art blossomed for a short time before the Soviets crushed the reforms of the Prague Spring in August of 1968. After twenty more years of normalization, Slovakia experienced enormous changes in the 1990s with the fall of the Berlin Wall. The changes resulted in fundamental shifts in literary expression.

Along the revival of "forbidden poets" from communist times, modernism and post-modernism swept the country; poetry became fragmented, decomposed; with evolving technology also less personal, but reflective of the search for a new identity. While this trend continues in the 21st century's postmodernist times, there are also new voices that gravitate back to natural lyricism or go the opposite direction—radical voices criticizing the society, pointing to environmental problems—and it is difficult to point out one prevailing style. Within his concept of palintropic philosophy, author and philosopher Erik Markovič formulates the need to transcend postmodernism and suggests a unified view of contemporary literature in Slovakia. In his words, "palintropicism is not only an effort to reach wholeness, unity, holistic metaphors of the world, but on a personal level, it is an expression of attempts for realized creative bridging of poetic, musical, and philosophical creating inside of the person as an author."

It is truly remarkable how diverse Slovak poetry is—while it may be caused by a span of generations and regime changes, I believe it is the creative expression of individual authors who do not compromise and do not imitate anybody but stay true to themselves.

Poetry has the power to reveal entire worlds in a few lines. My intention as the editor was to present a multitude of styles, to show how Slovak poets play with the language, transcending their experience beyond the words, into an unknown area that can be clarified and digested in the reader's mind.

The first poem in this collection questions the nature of a poem. In Slovak, the word "poem"—"báseň"—has a feminine grammatical gender, which evokes the association of a girl who is whimsical and hard to get. Two themes run throughout the following texts—the identity of a poem and the poetic or personal identity of authors. Mixed in are also themes of language, writing, and existential questions. Readers may enjoy beautifully crafted lyricism of Ondreička or Ondrejková, admire imagery in Luka, Podracká or Štrpka, wonder about author's experiences with Haugová, Repka, Kuniak, appreciate the boldness of Habaj and Pain. Other poems, like the ones from Dianišková, Gavura, Markovič, dare to hypothesize and predict; with a question mark, of course.

The last poem "Enclosed" is a good conclusion and almost a definition of hopes in Slovak poetry:

I am thinking about how to get out
it seems it won't be as easy…

…as easy as for poets of Western Europe who are globally recognized and published? It seems that the contemporary Slovak poetry is trying to reach the world but few listen.

My hope is that this selection encourages a wider interest in Slovak poetry among English-speaking readers.

I would like to express my immense gratitude for a fruitful collaboration with these distinguished literary experts: Erik Markovič, who has provided many original collections of poetry from his extensive

personal library for me to read and choose from; Miriam Margala, whose impeccable reading and reviewing skills contributed to clarity and artistic rendition of each poem; and Sibelan Forrester, professor of Modern and Classical Languages at Swarthmore College and an active member of American Literary Translators Association (ALTA), who encouraged me to translate contemporary authors and put me in contact with *Atlanta Review* editors.

Nina Varon

How Is She

How is the poem before she gets written?
Is she young, naïve, does she want to know more,
Will she not wait by my pen to be bitten,
Or will she weave herself into my score?

I have nothing on her, she wanders around,
Whistles a tune, snaps her fingers,
I should trust myself, write her down,
I have bits of her in my palms.

Ján Buzássy

Slovak

The language is beautiful when it knows the accents
That sing and themselves are songs,
It is not suitable for battle cries,
Yearnful singing is a long weapon of maidens.

Through our modest rain the language is moist,
It smells nice, steams, and has nutrients
It is a reflection, a bar hoisted too high,
Save, it, Lord, keep it among the living ones.

Ján Buzássy

I Always Come Out of the Same Door

God often sits at my gate. Here and there he transfers his weight
from one leg to another, chases out the last memory
from underneath his fingernails. We got used to each other—
it was easier for him than me.
When he doesn't know where he should hide, and the temperature drops
to 18 Fahrenheit, he shrugs his shoulders and slides under the earth. If
there was no frost, he would be afraid
of getting soggy and leaving only a trace in small streams between
the eyes of people passing by.
A social worker finds him there, or even the entire
non-profit organization, perhaps two; naked, legs crossed,
with a frosty look.
He would even pray to those up there if he were not God himself.

Veronika Dianišková

not quite alone...

the shadows of women
that I could/should have become
keep watch over me
but for various reasons I've never become them
although their image has
deeply embedded itself onto my retina:
multiplied looks, multiplying of the mind,
of hesitation, fears, but also of joy, desires, hopes...
especially on days full of misery
the shadows of the other
never realized women walk next to me,
sometimes they shine light under my floundering feet

Etela Farkašová

basic uncertainty

I don't know
how much uncertainty one poem can carry, how much melancholy
and sadness
as not to fall apart under too heavy a burden
ending in tatters without any meaning…

and I don't know at all
how much painful load does a human soul endure
heavily trudging/wading through a bog
when hopeless slimy mud sticks to its feet

Etela Farkašová

fatherline

my father stands at my bed
his shoulder touches emptiness
his skin is pearly soft
from skin holes
mustache sprouts   cat's claws
always catch my dress's hem
when I am in danger of flying too high

he stays at my bed
swaying

and the air suddenly undulates
The waves thickening into a jelly

                  he opens his mouth
      in them
                  a woman with the eyes of ice
                  an old woman without legs
                  they knead a child
                  they pour water on hot
                  sheet

one glance at my father's face
one touch the gate closes
the lips come together the shoulder leans
against the wall
                  they stand behind my back
                  creasing the hem of my dress

Mária Ferenčuhová

motherline

since childhood I have been spotting shadows in the corners of rooms
small animals on the surface of things
fast gray mice on the kitchen counter
insect with a multitude of little legs
my world was disappearing under the layers of other worlds
I was not surprised
if sometimes a strange man in a brown hooded sweatshirt stood
in the doorway and when the vases changed
into skulls with empty eye holes
when suddenly the skin on my mom's face was gone and on my shoulder
fell a shower of wrist bones instead
of a caress

with trusting, I submitted myself
when it was my turn
thankful
that we are made so
that we would not recognize anything and sensed
the end only as a transfer from one
environment into another   from a room to the hall
from darkness to light
                                   [or the other way]
and were afraid only of the fact
that we would not close the door behind

                    Mária Ferenčuhová

My Wise Friend

To keep quiet is treacherous,
As it is to crush
Butterflies.

All those majestic ones
With big wings
Like written thoughts
Of Socrates, crossed out
With a spot of blood and poison.
And also the ones of shadows and nights,
Covered only with grey fine hairs.

Open your mouth
And let the butterflies
Fly into a frosty December morning
Where I'll find them

On the sparkling snow, dried out
As an ink handwriting.

Ján Gavura

Profundis

Finally, the poetry is read sparingly,
Superficially and with the gesture of a Scrooge.

From the learning more secretive
Than a Masonic lodge
Grew apprenticeship of futility.

Only few remain who search for
Reflections of rhymes in the eyes of others,
In rhythmic steps a metaphor jumps
from one thing to another.

The one you write for is long dead
Or has not been born yet.
For now, only you are here.

Finally, the poet is alone.
Finally, he is himself.

Ján Gavura

1.

< | enter | >

the first sentence: doesn't have a central being. the first being: doesn't
have a central sentence. therefore one should not wonder there is
nothing to lean on. there is no center. there is nowhere to move. there
is no center. there is nothing to bounce back from. there is nothing to
follow. there is no being. there is no center. there is nothing to
estimate. the first center: doesn't have a being. doesn't have edges.
there is nothing to fit into. there is nothing to step over. there is no
center. there is nothing to discard. there is no sentence.

Generator X

26.

return. return. cyclization.
near the sea an irrelevant sea:
wind turns the pages of this text:
a future text or its medium:

on the ship deck an irrelevant ship deck:
someone checks the programming of this text:
a future text or its medium:

it begins and ends in a very descriptive way:
unreachable forgotten St. Ivan:
today a horizon.

| > exit < |

Generator X

ethnoshop:

the third world that has been us for a long time
the third world we are all in one
the third world of frozen poverty

citrus fruits
from Dutch genofarms
in a white stomach
caramel tobacco
in the saliva of a white man
banana in chocolate
in lip-rouged lips
bizarre fruit in winter
coffee and corn
coconut and cocaine
wooden rosaries
and sandalwood sticks
the third world built up by its denotation
impoverished by the supermarket
of a white man
by shopping carts
by philosophizing at universities

the biomass of the third world
in a reversed move
following the order of the unabomber
let them take currency corpus christi

out of circulation
the world is covered by the white spots
of white men's leprosy

take corpus christi out of circulation
touch my wound doubting Thomases
in the third world it has grown bigger
touch my wound
supermarket Judases
with 57 satellite channels

that feature a white man's poem
about hatred of the color white…

this poem?
this hatred?
this white?

Generator X

Name (Age)

she has never stopped wondering
how tiny
every little poem
about a person is

Ol'ga Gluštíková

Gabika (43) To Svetlana (38):

look what everybody around is
yelling at us:

how much you should make
how much to spend
what to accomplish
whom to marry and how to live with him
and meanwhile they do not tell you at all
that the human body
is soft

as bread

ripped out of the earth
for only a short moment

Ol'ga Gluštíková

Writer Elena (48)

I.
they are asking me what my
next books will be about:

about time and my mouth
with first dead teeth

about how during one night I
had sewn a wedding dress from curtains,
it was too long

about what kind of daughters
numismatic women have

about bathing a child and a mother
who resembled father

II.
they are asking me what will be left after us:
imperfect period cycles
wigs
red manuscripts:

after a home birth
the child wrapped in
a kitchen towel

Ol'ga Gluštíková

1805

I see scribbling, her blinking letters, she usually writes at night.

Now, when the letters fade, she goes to the curtain, children boast
"we saw her at the window in the morning."

Around Amherst a winding road, created for bundling.

Remove lines, plus signs, prefer "instant"
to "sudden," stick a red and white thread into places
with thick holes.

A bit of breeze from the window and the face clears up, *her flat, full lips
and dark eyes were not exactly masculine, her oval face and
low forehead are not exactly feminine.*

It is not true that I loved women, I loved everyone.

Erik Jakub Groch

Mise-en-scene

to write the time, long, incomprehensible sentences

it is possible to dream even of animals in a calendar

to hear once and for all the heaped crows from košice

word selection is a natural selection

: it doesn't matter how the universe was created

Erik Jakub Groch

Karmacoma

(1.)

Ashy faces do not foretell anything
In another country you perhaps know your name
You touch the sky with hair that does not belong to you
Whoever says hello to you leaves without a word
You don't belong anywhere
Ageless and getting younger still
You won't move forward if you misstep
And you will lose balance between two steps
Between two blades of grass in the wind
You are a sudden word that a long-forgotten language accepted
You are just the cry of a mute sky
That touches you with stars that do not belong to it
Whom does this dream belong to
The one in which you stumble and stand in one place
And ask about
Addresses names numbers the future
Destiny has lost balance between two lives
Ashy faces foretell nothing
You know that already
You spit in your palms
You'll never do that
You know your name now
In another country in another time in another future
Those birds land on your hands a mute sky cries from them
You are tearing the hair that does not belong to you
You screwed up addresses names futures
You mixed up steps words languages
You mixed up faces hair destinies
You don't belong anywhere
You had thousands of mothers thousands of fathers
Thousands of women thousands of daughters thousands of sons
In another future in another past
You don't belong anywhere
You don't belong anywhere
Bored, the Cosmos destroyed you

Michal Habaj

Karmacoma

(2.)

A very simple poem
You feel like saying
But the words are so heavy
You never saw such words
Where did those words come from
They are strange not known black creeping in the night
Bodies that they took off from ooze on the porch
Those words are wild unruly they are intelligent they are cold
Heavy, they sneak through the hall they entered the house
They entered the room the head they are in the head
Now what
You raise your hands you throw your hands onto the keyboard
You throw your hands you rip those words you grasp those words by
          nothing
by black wet nothing you rip words throw words
Out of the head
Out of the head
These are the words common dust
Lightly swirled dust nothing more
You feel like saying
But something sneaks through the night something entered the house
Something scrambles in the nearby hall
You never saw such words
Where did those words come from
You feel like saying
But the words say that for you
Task accomplished the area conquered
Such horrible intelligence is breathing
Who are you now
Who is asking
Hands on the keyboard write something

Michal Habaj

somewhere here. (un)certain dawn of the "text"

now. when the meaning in the infinite space of pure things
without names pushes me out, when I fall through in that vortex,
I live. in every word. that I become conscious of.
and which I grasp.
in an Abrasion: suddenly I. "I" in an abyss, wedged in the interplay
of new differences, silent through the nostrils full of dust.

the pressure in myself transcends the sign:
(resist the spice of binarity, the power cult!) in the space of a parabola
and a vertical, spider's net where the consciousness truly IS:
a sign in a manuscript thus leaks from every text
into another: the boundary is smeared, I breathe again, the time

net is dissolving, only a moment remains: now. and coming up to the
surface, a breath in, to see. myself. this way. from every side,
to step towards myself from the outside of a bubble (in which THAT I
decomposes and): only the fullness of clear breathing,
loneliness in a naked stone, smooth glance.

placed in the silky vacuum of vegetation.

Andrej Hablák

I am

the echo of the big bang is present
on smooth bridges, roads
breathe here. yes. You-not-know-it-all,
still a cold wind. slow glance. palm moving away
the echo of the big bang is present,
the sphere full of all movements seeps through my fiber
still the wave full of outlines sticks to my head. that deafens
on green platforms. on the bottoms of seeds light bursts forth

Andrej Hablák

(To My Poets-Peers)

In a forgotten house
invisibly but clearly
one can hear the rain
it resonates in the wintry foliage;
they photographed you at the first communion
in front of the old church in the May sun
an apple tree twig in your hair — — —
the house from a dream an opened door
windows colorless frames a slanted ray
in broken glass a brick fence
disappearing under the thin fingers of rain
wind children decrepit plaster
mold pastel spots
infinite childhood early adulthood
merge outside of my body deep inside me
the shadows of trees the warmth
prepared for a long winter I touch
the scarred light the cold sun
filters through the boy's
fingers on my face scantily
in the midst of future plants
grows a heart of shadow
unbuttons smoldering foliage firm shiny
herbs will encircle the house well entwined
roots reflected by a mirror the house
is undeniably standing here with you
and without you
definitively mature — —

Mila Haugová

Another Poem

Forever in an embrace, so gladly she welcomes the day, lets warm rays
enter the ancient forest of sleep,
she welcomes a poem, that very lively sister-twin
that is moving freely in her
and which she, to withstand the night and the shadow,
always kills in the evening with another poem.

Mila Haugová

Carnival

a face without a cause your young face
in the left upper corner of the painting

she is carrying all masks already
completely vulnerable
the carnival—a grille not one face of ours
will push through I have to do even what I did not want to
I want even what I cannot want
and so my hair grows now without you securing the footprints
I know only this embrace, no other
in my body I have another secret body folded gold scrolls
changing surfaces as they
submerge and emerge
walk close and open through me through my life
come up the stairs
towards the gold foil of the sky falling on us

Mila Haugová

Punctured Memory

I found out
that I have a punctured memory
but it functions
on the principle of the black hole
thus
it pulls everything inside
backwards
it absorbs
and so I remember strange names
                    strange numbers
                    strange troubles
                    strange loves
I keep in my memory
uncles aunts grandmothers girlfriends
ID numbers of hometowns
of the entire city and also county
I am like an information service
a public phone booth
do not destroy me I serve all
while I forget
even my own name
and also what I wanted
to say here

Daniel Hevier

Ministry of My Interior

Who again was
searching me through?
The Ministry
of My Interior.

All my teeth
they have inspected,
if my heart loves
they have detected,

(they have warned me
with a smile
that my heart
won't make a mile)

they have fixed
my tonsils' order,
liver might be
getting harder...
Then they passed
straight from my head
into stomach
acid ache:

how many acids
I have, bases.
If I still have
all my graces.

A threat of the highest
punishment for me:
life sentence
in my own skin.

Daniel Hevier

Casting a Look

Tired, I am coming home from work,
nothing exists yet—
only when I open my eyes:
By casting a look
I spread the sidewalk under my feet,
unearth a tree,
by casting a look,
I spread the sky,
blow a cloud on it
and the sun.

Rudolf Jurolek

Anytime

I live. Just so, without engagements,
just so, with hands in my pockets:
anytime I can listen to music,
anytime I can do something good,
anytime I can make a somersault.

I live. Just so, without engagements,
just so, with hands in my pockets:
anytime a car can run me over,
anytime I can get a heart attack,
anytime I might not exist.

I live.
So much on the interface
of everything and nothing
that I freeze sometimes.

Rudolf Jurolek

Normal Children

As our children are growing out
of plump new-born shapes,
our disappointments are multiplying:
those are not the children
we dreamt of—
they have crooked teeth,
fat noses,
eyes of uncertain color,
they don't stun the adults
with their smart answers.
They will not become the prodigies
that are always successful in life:
they will have to earn money,
their loves will leave them,
they won't be able to sleep at night.
Children are growing out
of plump new-born shapes
and with their imperfections
they gain
always the deeper and touching
dimension of simple humanity.

Rudolf Jurolek

There are unique places in every person's life.

Not too many. According to Laco Lajčiak: A place where a person
is from, where he spent his childhood. According to Laco Faga: A
place where person lives. According to Ján Kudlička: A place in a
landscape. I understand all three and I believe that MY unique place
is equivalent to theirs, even when I have not been born there and live
elsewhere, surrounded by a different landscape.

Juraj Kuniak

A point.

During flights on big planes to very remote countries, every
passenger's seat is equipped with a screen, on which various films
and information about the flight are being broadcasted, for example,
the map of an area the plane is flying over is displayed, and the icon
of the plane draws a red line—so that everyone can see how far we
have flown already and where we are flying. I have flown like that
many times, noticing these orientation points, *Wien, Warszaw,
Moscow or Singapore, Sydney, Tahiti*, and have also noticed that
such a point is not always the country's capital. Sometimes it was
an entirely different place. Suprisingly different. For example, there
is a point marked on our country's map close to the border of the
eastern Slovakia with Hungary, with the name *Cana* next to it. The
east-Slovakian village of Čaňa. As a native of Košice I know this
village. For some, Čaňa might be unique and takes a central part in
his soul. I personally would mark another place. I would put a point
in the northern middle part of Slovakia and write *Cernova* next to it.

Juraj Kuniak

Addition

I stay away from people and prefer to count the birds—
crazies look at me—the madman—and sneer at him.
So why should I be with them in cahoots?
Little birdies will sum up my deeds without a grin.

Ján Litvák

Happiness

Immense happiness came my way this morning,
like when the first sunrays through leafy woods are shining.
Today, I am content and will stay at home.
I feel like being alone.

Ján Litvák

Language of Languages

How many languages can heavenly birds sing in
when they praise tidied-up gardens and yards.
I suddenly understand them involuntarily
when you speak to me so lovingly.

Ján Litvák

Deepgreen Woman

She comes in quietly
and with little drums in her wrists
You sense their disquiet under the fragile apple skin
A voice sleeps in her throat
                        A warm hairy animal
And all that blinking nostalgia!

She breathes on the flower
The flower shivers in carnality just like after a bitter rain
All ambience calms down
                        and flickers light
A deepgreen woman with lit up hair
touches bird nests and thinks
of mirrors and grievances
                        of forgotten jungles

In the country of her body
in the shell of her silence
                        somebody is making wings to fly

Eva Luka

A Poet

Like animals sniff the secret holes
of their bodies on each other, so does the lover's hand
approach the white paper, weaves in
its foreplay, on the aorta the scythe of the moon
like a shivering scarf, a frog's membrane
among his fingers
that he hides at noon.

Only this night
can see him, impossible and sad
hanging on a branch, swinging and asking for nothing
all those useless, complicated questions. Drunk
on cheap wine, he sleeps all night, gorgeous
poems fly into his hair and they will never
see the light of the day. Such
strange trivialities. The bird man

very quietly plays on his street organ, blows off a thin
hair from his face and disappears

in a grievous pirouette.

Eva Luka

7 Everyday Situations

The idea that someone heard our voice
while the door was closed,
is, honestly, filling us with feelings
of uncertainty. Let's imagine it.

Let's imagine it thus: the person who
suggested this had heard the voices from our room,
he thought that he recognized them as ours,
but he is not sure—it could have been a
a radio playing.

It's even possible that we weren't there
but our radio was playing:
someone else turned it on.

But it is not entirely excluded
that we were there, but the radio wasn't playing.

That evening we were there,
at the agreed place,
in a clearly defined space.
Or the radio was playing.

If we weren't there and the radio was not playing,
then their assumption was wrong,
it is not true that someone heard us.
Let's hope we existed that evening.

Even then, if someone really talked
in our room, even when we weren't there
and the radio was turned off.

Peter Macsovzsky

Ec chajim.

And that something like this can still happen again, we could not
have even imagined anymore. Moonikonika

And if You cannot imagine it—
that not only the dark cattle wagons once approaching the smoke,
but all the trains roaming the world are like torn pieces of some epic movie,

where the idea of winding film rolls is similar
and somehow unconsciously derived from winding the Torah scroll *Ec chajim*
on two wooden bars as a symbol of the Tree of Life.—

And if You really cannot imagine it,
please try to see the just setting Sun as the reflector of a film projector,
in a movie theatre that the Gestapo or NKVD* burst in to seize

a forbidden film, ripped it to pieces and sent everybody to be transported,
trains as scraps of an epic film that the setting Sun plays forever
like a movie projector during an eclipse.

And if You really could never imagine it, please remember,
what I was telling You that not the ages, but people started to be vulgar,
when I told You that before the outbreak of the

Holocaust first the language and people's speech were becoming vulgar, also lies,
remember, please, how I was telling You this, all of it only a few years ago,
that all of this precedes

war, even if others looked at me like I was a crazy idiot,
please remember how I was telling You that;
but also to You when I didn't suspect yet that You would start swearing too,

which I almost did not survive, remember that I was saying all of this when
nobody could have known or even suspected—unimaginable until then—
that in a few years a war in Ukraine would really finally break out.

As it is written: by thoughts, words, deeds.
Try, I beg You very much, to imagine that the excerpts and scraps of the epic film
in the form of trains are not lit up during an eclipse by lights, but by the reflector

of the setting Sun shining through them and thus illuminating them,
and even if the Holy Spirit blows these scraps around the earth surface as it wishes,
not only our every deed but also the tiniest move and the most tranquil word,

a thought or only its suggestion, and inner stirring—
they will never be lost in gas or in the smoke of the burning night or otherwise,
but all of this will be sooner or later visibly and intensely projected

through us, illuminated in trains—
truly all the way to heaven.

(written in 2014-15, published in magazine *Fraktál* 2020/4)

Erik Markovič

Note:
*NKVD = from Russian (Narodnyj komissariat vnutrennich del), Soviet secret police
agency, whose original goal was to root any potential opposition to Stalin by means of mass
arrests, show trials, and executions. Forerunner of KGB.

Palintropicity and the Concept of Postmodernism in the Current Slovak Literature (An Attempt at Another of the Theoretical Parts of the Past-Postmodern Manifesto)
2010 (extracts)

(...) Based on what I've seen, postmodernism is mostly disappearing from Slovak literature. It used to be influential and creative, but now it's running out of ideas. So, if we want to be innovative, we'll have to move beyond postmodernism.

(…) Most people are not aware of the situation, except for a few isolated cases. They don't have a clear negative or positive feeling towards it. I'm not talking about occasional criticism or texts based on postmodern principles. I'm talking about the lack of clear statements either supporting or opposing postmodernism. We can't fully accept or reject postmodernism. Ignoring recent history would be a mistake, but embracing it is unrealistic. Yet, we can try to understand postmodernism to some extent. We can talk about the good parts of postmodernism without accepting or rejecting it. We should approach postmodernism critically and differentiate between extreme positions. This should be the starting point for further discussion and understanding.

(...) Palintropicity offers a unique perspective on postmodern literature and its connection to postmodernity. It is an effort graded in several steps. The palintropic concept tries to explain postmodern writing in a theoretical manifesto. It aims to go beyond post-modern writing.

(…) When we say palintropic transcending postmodernism, we mean that we go beyond it. We also come from the postmodern era. This leaves behind something that needs more explanation. We don't completely reject all past postmodernism. Instead, we transform specific cultural traditions that we choose. Our goal is not to immediately stop postmodernity, but to make it better and move to a higher level. It's a slow process that only affects certain parts of postmodernism.

(...) Palintropicism is a way to achieve wholeness on a personal level. It involves creating poetry, music, and philosophy that connects the author's thoughts and emotions.

(...) This created space-time renews the world's faith. The proposed palintropics express it. Oculus Mundi is a dome that surrounds us. It is the world's temple with the sun as a lantern and its pupil. Oculus Mundi is also Oculus Dei, the eye of God that contains us all.

(...) This attempt will replace networks with postmodernity. We understand postmodernity as dispersed amorphous power. It is a structured retina being. The retina being is both an embodied idea and a schematic idea. It bends the ontological difference between being and being. If I shall answer the final questions, one places oneself on the flexible retina of the eye of God. This happens in a literary and ontological space. They call this light *Lichtung des Seins*, aletheia, unclosedness, which acts like a sun visor to the higher world.

Erik Markovič

Summary
In his study, author at first tries to follow upon the concept of four key points in the development of Slovak literature, which was formulated by P. Zajac. According to the concept, the current situation in Slovak literature could be characterized as waiting for the fifth key point. The author tries to outline and argue that his proposed concept of so called palintropic philosophy could be one of the concepts that could contribute to the gradual formation of the fifth key point. It is an attempt to create a philosophically argued position of extra-postmodernistic and post-postmodernistic writing. The text also suggests how palintropic philosophy could relate to the Lyotardean, Foucaultean, and Deleuzean line of postmodernistic thinking about literature.

les femmes fatales

women that spread sheets for men in coffins
women born out of incest like divinity
women in skin
women tortured by other women in cold blood
women swimming in the darkness of foamed salt
women leeches with sensitivity for pain
women bleeding from the scar in their lap
women in men
women morbidly desiring the touch of women
women in white red and black
women passionately faking orgasms
women feeding dogs flesh from breasts
women with trophies
women with a plastic penis in a box under the bed
women reviving the sense of craziness
women a nightmare of the count de sternenhoch
women putting a curse on their fathers
women in pants
women in bordellos with viper evil eyes
women flexible as the limbs of an arrow
women Amazonians
women queens evoking passion in agony
women worshipers of sleeping pills and abortions
women obsessively grown together with horses
women put to sleep by the fairy tales of psychiatrists
women in posthumous masks
women murdering sons shortly after the birth
women that fornicate only with the dead

Marián Milčák

with a light feeling of shame

without portals and candles
without saying goodbyes in the front room
not guarded
with a light feeling of shame
the dead one is disappearing from our eyes

in the sterile hall of an autopsy room
in awe he looks at the body
after the expiration date on the bed of ice

he awaited an angel
and a man in green entered
a face mask on his mouth underneath
a smile (sauna love-making
with a nurse last-night basketball
seven baskets beer)

in his soul a routine peace
in his hands by now an unnecessary
surgical precision

Marián Milčák

the lord of the text

go in already
the door is open

no need to knock
no need to be afraid
that it is too late

no need to explain
anything

i rule here
the death has no access
to the text

after the revolt
of the tropics after the coup of political figures
history lost
its power

similarily chaos

time and circumstance are overcome
by only a minor patrol of verses
on any borders
of my world

Marián Milčák

How to

How to accept the gift
of decline and watch the grass
at the same time, which repeats itself
carelessly; how to buy the unchained joy back
from the hands of a man who is walking away
from himself; how to stand
at the start line without trembling
that is only the mirror of the mind
welcoming nothingness, always suddenly
present, itself curled in its own shivers
that needs to be in the steady moment hugged, cuddled,
wrapped in a warm blanket and then further
I can ponder how

Peter Milčák

5 Times Perfection

The perfection of silence
the perfection of flowers
the perfection of breathing
by a prayer-answered sentence

the perfection of light
in the somber shadows of dusk
when it joins the river of black
in its words-on-paper flight

the perfection of a ball of wool
that from our hands reels off`
and opens an abyss full
of space named nothingness

Erik Ondrejička

1. perfection (catching silence)

Silence is caught
easiest at twilight
when the day and night
have an even fight

and trees point out
with a silenced breath
where that peaceful veil
shall come down from
filled with quietness
from taciturn stars

and the forest stretches nets
from the darkening air
and immovably awaits
the silence to land in the ear

and the connectedness
of silence catch
on the edges of moss
and in primordial grasses

until someone somewhere
from that silence
releases its taste

A taste that is only fanciful
and can never be heard
in words

Erik Ondrejička

2. the absolute (flower)

They separate
coarseness from the fineness
until the refinement in them
is perfectly purest
like the past
from a future virtue
in emerald tablet
of Hermes Trismegistus

and in every curve
and in all the creases
they hide everlastingness
of all the moments

also that the thorn is
mostly spiky and thin
also that temporality
its petals cannot pin

and only ostentation
compares to them
such as when the grass
wishes to reach the sun

but when the perfection
truly mature is
color, shape, and scent
to the flower it gives

Erik Ondrejička

From a Distance

Mommy, my mouth is hurting
when I read your letter aloud.

I stand on a river bank
and cannot wade through
so I could taste
your bread.

Long time ago did the festive chandeliers
of chestnut trees wither,
the only ones left here for me.

Mommy, sadness flows through my bones
as if they were the ashes
of linden twigs,
that the wind carries away.

Mommy, here burn
little lanterns with my blood
in the black valleys of towns.

Mommy, I dreamt that
the sun burst into primroses
and flew towards me like the rain,
when I returned to you.

I am stepping into the river barefooted…

Anna Ondrejková

Lie interruptus

2/ house arrest

A flower from a man, / whom
you don't love
/, a woman, /
thank-you comes later / First
the master and then / the prophet-executioner /
a feathered singer / Spanish bird   / sings a swan song /
hatha-
titla / /
Damn the whole world / a poisonous caterpillar
already
gathers in the throat / like a hairy
word /
A woman that doesn't love / / on the cross
two gallows / silence
bells toll the night / tear away
from the dream / pinkish lids
/ on sterile non-conscience / atom
mushroom pickers whipping / Boy
on the bed /
kiss me,
/ says the woman who doesn't love me

Agda Bavi Pain

Oath

To spit out the soul: / into palms
/ to clap / / to yourself
you heard//nothing / you saw
nothing / do not speak /
/ but I will beat it
out of myself

Agda Bavi Pain

Untitled (and I love the tree with pure love)

and I love the tree with pure love
I do not want anything from it
it does not want anything from me
a bird is flying between us
between the whispering of the leaves
and the silence of the mind
we are joined only
in the flight of a bird
whispering in silence
the wind agrees

Daniel Pastirčák

Untitled (one eye looks out from its blindness)

one eye looks out from its blindness
it stares: he is not there
the second eye looks into its blindness
it stares: he is there

God dances in that blindness
he smiles from one eye to the other
He sings
I see myself with one eye
with the other, I don't see myself

Daniel Pastirčák

Untitled (just to be)

just to be
not for nor against
not to be a person
only space
through which you walk
towards me through me
in between me in me
beloved enemy
falling on you
in a silent rain
dropping from your lashes
on the lips full of
curses
without hatred without affection
warmly and without presence like the sun
only to be present for you
in the one who is
and never comes close
and never leaves

Daniel Pastirčák

Theology of Ascension. Rúfus

The cell where he was a creator:
a tonsure of light, a pulpit and a cross,
nothing more

Pascha is in the mind, it's enough to transfer awareness
from a smaller world into a bigger, one
to be swallowed by the Existence

Totus Tuus
He is all Yours

And in Him
a girl with Down Syndrome
gulps the light by spoonfuls
at the highest level
in excelsis

Lifting that little girl is enough
and the flight of the lonely her to the lonely him
ascends to the rupturing ceiling,
opening an aperture

The end cannot be seen,
Who's uplifting whom
whether the father his daughter or the daughter her father

Pieta is in motion

Dana Podracká

Untitled (The fog enveloped the sun and bright colors)

The fog enveloped the sun and bright colors,
    snow was falling—a bit too early.

I can be (only)
your silent
poem.

A happy exclamation point,
a sad exclamation point,
a gentle triple-colon;

with a sentimental beast behind the back.

Stanislava Chrobáková Repar

Untitled (Frost)

Frost,
hibernation.
Norse on a horse

"My little soul is asking
how is your little soul doing."

Greet the forest and pet the snow,
hug the playful landscape. Breathe on
my heart, like I do on yours... I would like to
watch your motion, the bending line of your body

on a sparkling snow on the hill.

And peek again into your life.

And dive with you to the bottom.

Stanislava Chrobáková Repar

Eternal Life

There will be time when I won't comb the sand out of my hair
on the road through liquid dunes.

I will become a permanent boat
on the shore.

The light of your lamp
 swings on the waves.

/1972/

Peter Repka

Running, Like Every Movement, Takes Away What We Had

1
Come, let's run.
Let's enter the houses
that will be burnt at night.

Bloody September
in the heart.

We floated in the sky,
children waved at us
from a blue train:
Hi, runners!

2
Now I go to run only
when everybody sleeps.

Alone in myself
and a day in a day.

The lonely of the world, unite!*

Amen

Peter Repka

Note:
*This sentence exemplifies Marx and Engel's Communist Manifesto and its motto:
Workers of all countries, unite! Repka is using it in this poem to express the atmo-
sphere of the 70s. Replacing "workers" with "lonely", he associates himself with the
"Lonely Runners" (Osamelí bežci), a group of poets (Repka, Štrpka, Laučík) active in
the 1960s through the 1980s and beyond.

It Goes Anywhere

The planet of my eye flies through the moving universe
and the rest of the body, formed around it,
has a lot to do to follow its gravitation.

In the sand, the visible unceasing presence
of improvising grains

Spreading anywhere,
while it is possible to maintain the variable balance of the stream
it carries forward!

Those who fainted won't stumble anymore from the grain to the
stone, not even on the stilts of crosses.

Examples of summersaulting apples are of interest to many,

secretly spying
their own fight for survival.

The best of them becomes a predator
that by the claws of black seeds
reaches for the center
and still cannot quite grasp the age of giants.

So self-involved it cannot actually notice
the growing stems of grass
that help each other grow tall.

Martin Solotruk

A View as If From the Gut

How long will my feeling of being lost
last among the insides of the rockpile
when the hammer, the hammer
and here the heart so exactly interpret the opinions of the majority?

They need a point they would latch onto,
even if it was a falling star
that divides the horizon into the hidden and the obvious.

Many smiles then fight
for their spot in the light.

Completely outside of myself a telephone rings, it inspects
whether I am in the correct position,
such as the one that I deserve for a few moments of concentration,

soon without the cord…
…the clouds pass, each one with a different joy from colors,
each one with its own human, each unique at the meeting.

The human experiences friendship this way
already in the belly.
The time of catching colors starts at the first moment
and you too are back in the grass,
rolling around

and sometimes, without the feeling of guilt,
you wail with your feet over something unforgivable.

Martin Solotruk

Where Is That Door?

We are (perhaps) that thing which is
inside and outside at the same time. To the extent
when inside and outside (for us)
ceases to be (divided).
To be outside does not mean
not to be inside. Outside voices are not
only inside. We are not only
inside (what we are). And we continue to
(always) clash with divided worlds
with each exhale and inhale.
The saints without baptism (also without
holiness)? Initiated only through
their own incessant fumbling: where
is it? Where is (that) door that
only has one side?
(Where is that door that
eliminates all the other) doors? (Where is)
that door, in which the light
hesitates? Where (is that
door), in which the laughter
itself also laughs?

Ivan Štrpka

Europe: a Slow Headache

The sun is setting and leaves
us with empty hands here.
On the other bank, the last reflection
of armor that gallops through the shadows
incessantly, always following the light,
is descending on rustling leaves.
The pounding is strong. The forms are empty.
And we are passing a child: a glittering
ball is falling in the water. Dizzily
sinking to the bottom. And never ends its fall.

Ivan Štrpka

The Fly is Sleeping

"These are the days when no one should rely on his competence.
Strength lies in improvisation. All the decisive blows
are struck left-handed'" says W.B. (1892-1940)*
on the eve of inevitable defeat of dark forces.
Breeze does not circle. The fly is sleeping
like a log. Rosenkranz and Guldenstern
are dead for ages. Chipped-off bases
of Dorian columns point back to unity.
I roam in the night house as a live ghost
of my father (1914-1997). Moonlight
enters through the curtainless window
onto the empty bed of my parents
with full force. A voice somewhere
inside my sleep without sleep also without dream
is still quietly ranting: grasp those unconscious
movements, take aim without aiming, just so
cut down tall fragile stalks without seed that
lead the spring growth. You will not fall asleep
before the dawn nor during the day. You will not
extinguish lime-wash in an empty palm.
You will not adhere. You will not whiten. You will not succumb to blindness
(you will not extinguish in the middle of an enormous
unextinct eye that follows brightness).
Spring is a blow: the fly is sleeping, world is giving birth,
the grave is bottomless and empty. Apple trees
give light and continue. Now
is the morning of the whole question.

Ivan Štrpka

Note:
*Walter Benjamin's quote

Manual Work Good Feeling

actually I have a good feeling when something gets done
the grass gets mowed the vineyard gets pruned the property and
poultry are tended to
the lunch gets cooked coffee made and then mineral water is a must
the house the office or solar dust get vacuum-cleaned
Pichler's stamped impressions get framed
the first and second pages get printed
a mushroom is picked and a basket gets new wildflowers
all the computers are connected etc.
but the fact is that I hate manual work
(doesn't matter that it is accompanied by happy music like in the
movies)
so I am now drinking, spinning a crystal glass
and I try to organize everything sitting on a bar stool
occasionally I think of sex and the direction of the world
of manual work and four proto robots
I write poems similar to this one
or the next one about the lives of tattooed dragons
or I am simply writing
and have a good feeling

a good feeling

perhaps

Peter Šulej

Enclosed

enclosed in a cycle
in spaces in buildings in cultures
in languages in blind windows
(of previously industrial facilities)
I am thinking about how to get out
it seems it won't be as easy
as opening a plastic bottle with sparkling mineral water
even if here too sometimes there is the danger of gushing out
of the loss of reason during violence and speed

Peter Šulej

Contributors

Erin Aube is a recovering attorney turned high school English teacher. Originally from a valley in Tennessee, she lives in Atlanta, Georgia, with her husband, Charlie and daughters Zelda and Marigold. Her work has appeared in *Poetry South, The Emerson Review, Door is a Jar*, and *UCity Review*.

Born and raised in Flowery Branch, Georgia, **Brittany J. Barron** graduated with her MFA in Creative Writing at Georgia College. Her poetry has appeared in *Plainsongs, The Examined Life Journal*, and *Poetry South*. Currently, she teaches at Florida State University, where she is a Ph.D. candidate in Rhetoric and Composition.

R. Steve Benson studied poetry with the late poet James Hearst at the University of Norther Iowa. Steve taught Art in Iowa schools for 33 years. His 46 ink drawings, illustrating phrases from poems by Dylan Thomas, were exhibited in Iowa City's Public Library. He's married with three children and two grandkids.

Ace Boggess is author of six books of poetry, most recently *Escape Envy*. His writing has appeared in *Indiana Review, Michigan Quarterly Review, Notre Dame Review, Harvard Review*, and other journals. An ex-con, he lives in Charleston, West Virginia, where he writes and tries to stay out of trouble.

Michele Bombardier is the 2024 winner of the NORward Prize. Her collection, *What We Do*, was a Washington Book Award finalist. Her work has appeared in *JAMA, Bellevue Literary Review, Parabola*, and others. She's a Hedgebrook and Tyrone Guthrie Centre fellow and the poet laureate of her town.

Grey Brown has three collections of poetry, *Staying In, When They Tell Me*, and *What It Takes*. She holds a Masters in English from NYU. Her poems have been published in *Greensboro Review, Blue Pitcher, Kakalak, Literary Trails of Eastern NC, JAMA* and others.

William Brown is a PhD student in poetry at Texas Tech University. His poems have appeared in journals such as *Copper Nickel, Crab Creek Review, The Hopkins Review, Tupelo Quarterly*, and elsewhere.

Intellectual metaphors with sensuous perception, free verse and sonnets, wide-ranging cyclical compositions, and delicate refined poetic miniatures—all these are the lasting features of **Jan Buzássy's** (b. 1935) poetry. Fascinated by ancient cultures in which he has found an aesthetic ideal: a balance of mind and feeling, a "sensitive intelligence and an intelligent feeling," Ján is a devoted poet.

Peter Neil Carroll recently published *This Land, These People: The 50 States* (2022), which won the Prize Americana; and *Talking to Strangers: poetry of everyday life* (2022). His poems have appeared in many literary journals. He is currently Poetry Moderator for Portside.org and lives in northern California.

Ann Chinnis lives in Virginia, is an Emergency Physician, and studies under Philip Schultz at the Writers Studio in New York. Her first chapbook, *Poppet, My Poppet*, is forthcoming from Finishing Line Press. She is published in *Speckled Trout Review, Sky Island Journal, Nostos,* and *Sheila-NA-Gig*, among others.

Chloe Cook holds a BA in English from Northern Kentucky University. Her writing is featured in *The Journal, Bayou Magazine, Arkansas Review*, and *Delta Poetry Review*, among others. She is currently an MFA student at the University of Florida.

Veronika Dianišková (b. 1986) studied dramaturgy and works as a teacher of theater and literature. Her original work is presented at events, in magazines, and through broadcasting on the radio. She likes to write when she is on the move, physically distant from her known environment, which enables her to tap into her inner resources and describe them as processes by using verbal impressionism and psychoanalytical language.

Holly Day's poetry has recently appeared in *Slipstream, Penumbric*, and *Maintenant*. She is the co-author of the books, *Music Theory for Dummies* and *Music Composition for Dummies* and currently works as an instructor at The Richard Hugo Center in Seattle and at the Loft Literary Center in Minneapolis.

Deborah H. Doolittle has lived in lots of different places, but now calls North Carolina home. Her recent publications include *Floribunda* and *Bogbound*. Some of her poems have appeared or will soon appear in *Comstock Review, Ibbetson Street, Iconoclast, Pinyon Review, Rattle, Slant,* and *The Stand*. An avid bird-watcher, she shares a home with her husband, six housecats, and a backyard full of birds.

Prose, poetry, essays, and translations produced by writer and philosopher **Etela Farkašová** (b. 1943) concentrate on the themes of women, family, intergenerational problems, ecology. Writing for Etela is about self-reflection, connection to the world, and a therapy. She is a member of SC PEN Club and established organizations for gender studies and women philosophers, among others.

Mária Ferenčuhová (b. 1975) studied film screenwriting and dramaturgy and contributes to multiple magazines in Slovakia and lectures at a university. As a poet, she is an exciting author who has been translated into many languages. Poetry for her is an experience on the edge and the poems have sources in her diaries. She features images as indexes of the world in her fragmented, imaginary, and beautiful poems, complemented by emotional discourse.

J.V. Foerster is a Pushcart nominated poet. Her book *Holy Mess of a Girl* also a mini chapbook *Truth or Consequences* were released in August 2023. She is published in many literary magazines. She has work in multiple anthologies. She lives in Ashland, Oregon.

Daniel Galef's first book, *Imaginary Sonnets*, is a collection of persona poems all from the point of view of different historical figures and objects, including Nossis the Epizephyrian, Christopher Smart's cat, and a breakfast taco. His flash fiction on J. Robert Oppenheimer was published in the *Best Small Fictions* anthology.

Ján Gavura (b. 1975) teaches versology, Slovak and world literatures of the 20th century in Prešov. His poetry is a cultivated and intimate expression of the search for cultural and esthetic values that last over the time. Based on mythological motives, the lyrical subjects in his poems are hunting but also yielding, being sensitive to sound and image.

A conglomerate of multiple authors, **Generator X** hides 4 authors: Maczovszky, Šulej, Habaj, and Hablák. It is also a name for an experimental poetry project, with its part featured in this presentation of Slovak poets.

Oľga Gluštíková (b. 1987) is a media specialist, poet and publicist, comes from Orava region in northern Slovakia. She studied journalism, wrote for the economic daily newspaper, and currently works for big construction and industrial companies. Her poems were translated into many languages and published in various media around the world. She is fascinated by femininity, nature, and symbiosis between humanity and landscape, in which the existence of one organism is conditioned by the other.

A wide selection of new poems by **Jeff Graham** has come out in the anthology: *Crystal Fire* (Moonrise Press 2022). Publications for 2023/24 include current and forthcoming appearances in journals such as *Iconoclast, California Quarterly, Haight Ashbury Literary Journal, Blue Unicorn,* and *The San Francisco Haiku Anthology: The Next 30 Years.*

Erik Jakub Groch (b. 1957) was a member of literary, art, and intellectual underground group Nace in Košice in the 1980s, publishing samizdat literature. Other than a poet, he is a publisher, editor, and a graphic designer. His sentences or verses float to the surface from his subconsciousness and memory. A poet-mystic, he connects nature with the need for human understanding and love, coming out of theo-physical tradition.

Employed at the Institute of Slovak Literature as a literary researcher, **Michal Habaj** (b. 1974) was awarded international prizes for poetry. In his own words, the real poetry has no choices; it is inevitable, like the roll of dice where the poet's task is to correctly interpret the numbers of destiny. Life experience and reconstruction of poetry with traditional and post-modernist elements is present in his work.

Andrej Hablák (b. 1977) is a teacher of Slovak language and literature philosophy, redactor, editor, literary critic. He worked as an editor in literary magazine *Romboid* and literary review *Pulz* in daily newspaper Pravda. He published 5 books of poetry: *Váhavo postavám nepripravený odísť,* 1995, *Jazyk,* 1999, *Ti horad,* 2002, *Leknin,* 2009, *Bahnokrvny,* 2019. In the present, he lives in Orava, northern Slovakia.

Bex Hainsworth is a poet and teacher based in Leicester, UK. Her work has appeared in *The McNeese Review, Honest Ulsterman, New Welsh Review, trampset,* and *bath magg. Walrussey,* her debut pamphlet of ecopoetry, is published by Black Cat Poetry Press.

Mare Heron Hake (she/her) lives in the Salish Sea region of Washington State. Until recently, Hake was poetry editor, co-owner, and co-publisher for *Tahoma Literary Review* and her work has recently appeared as a finalist for Terrain.Org's poetry contest. She has two books available in the usual places.

Mila Haugová (b. 1942) is a great dame of Slovak poetry with many literary prizes, and her poems have been translated into multiple languages. She is one of the most inspirational and prolific authors, who also translates and recreates the works of other famous poets. Her poems connect to the world of humans, animals, and plants, in search of humanity and caring for all living beings.

A popular writer of poems, children's literature, editor, publisher, **Daniel Hevier** (b. 1955) is also a pioneer of e-learning and courses of creative writing in Slovakia. He feels at home in various artforms—when he does not feel successful at writing, he paints or sings. As a universal creative personality, he is also very original and has a sense of humor that is appreciated by his readership.

Joanne Holdridge lives in Devens, MA, but spends as much of the winter as she can on skis in northern NH. She has published poems in a wide variety of publications, including a previous issue of *Atlanta Review*, and been nominated four times for a Pushcart Prize.

Paul Ilechko is a British American poet and occasional songwriter who lives with his partner in Lambertville, NJ. His work has appeared in many journals, including *The Bennington Review, The Night Heron Barks, deLuge, Stirring*, and *The Inflectionist Review*. He has also published several chapbooks.

Donald Illich has published poetry recently in *The MacGuffin, Slant,* and *Okay Donkey*. His book is *Chance Bodies* (The Word Works, 2018). He lives and works in Maryland.

Tess K. Jacobs is a writer, folklorist, and visual artist. She holds a PhD in English with an emphasis in folklore studies from Ohio State University. Her illustration work has appeared in *She Vote*s (2020). She currently resides in Munich, Germany.

Siobhan Jean-Charles (she/her) graduated with her Bachelor's from Salisbury University and is an MFA candidate at Arizona State University. Her work has appeared in *Tinderbox Poetry Journal, The Tusculum Review, Furrow, Broadkill Review, The Shore*, where she is the blog editor, and elsewhere.

P M F Johnson has won The Brady Senryu Award from The Haiku Society of America, been short-listed for The Touchstone Award, and won Honorable Mention in *The Atlanta Review* International Poetry Contest. His poems appear in *Evansville Review, Nimrod, North American Review, Poetry East, Threepenny Review*, and elsewhere.

Rudolf Jurolek (b. 1956) studied mechanical engineering, but worked as a teacher, journalist, and publisher. He likes to be succinct in his poetry, motivated to express his reconstruction of the world in intimate, introspective wandering. Nature is an exemplar of simplicity, which he follows in his poems. Rudolf previously lived in the Orava region in northern Slovakia and currently lives and works in Trnava.

Juraj Kuniak (b. 1955) is a poet, writer, translator, former constructor, mountaineer and businessman, founder, and editor of Skalná ruža (Rock Rose) publishing. He has published more than 20 books of various genres, but his main domain remains poetry. The author of ten poetry collections is perceived as a poet of the country and global problems. He translates from American poetry (Whitman, Hass) and lives in central Slovakia in the mountain village of Kordíky.

Sophie Liebergall writes from Philadelphia, PA, where she is pursuing an MD-PhD degree in Neuroscience and counting out haikus as she jogs along the river trail. Her poetry and prose have been published in *Third Wednesday Magazine* and *apenndx*.

Jessica Lim is a Pākehā, Chinese-Indonesian poet, curator and archivist. She holds a Masters in Sociology (First). Her poetry can be found in the anthology *A Clear Dawn* (AUP, 2021) and the literary journals *Starling, Sweet Mammalian, Takahē*, and *Dreamcatcher*. She currently lives in London. @jessicalim.tv

Ján Litvák (b. 1965) is a poet, editor, and a translator, a member of literary group Barbaric Generation. He translated, among others, works of Arthur Rimbaud, William Blake, and Julien Barnes. Since 2013, he is the editor-in-chief of the monthly magazine *At Home in the Garden*. He was born and lives in Bratislava and values authors who are able to express the essentials without a need to compete.

Eva Luka (b. 1965) is a highly sought translator and interpreter from Japanese. Her poetry is magical, emanating nostalgic cruelty, captivating images, playing with gender roles and words in masterful texts. Dramatic and emotional language of the poems reflect her deep personal experience with life and death to the point when readers do not have the words to answer this mesmerizing creativity.

Jenny Maaketo (she/her) is a neurodivergent writer, psychiatric nurse, former professional actor, and poetry candidate in the MFA Creative Writing program at the University of Mississippi. She was named a semifinalist in the 2023 Crab Creek Review Poetry Prize, a finalist in the 2023 Michelle Boisseau Poetry Prize, and runner-up in the 2022 Patty Friedmann Writing Competition.

Peter Macsovszky's (b. 1966) jobs included being a teacher, editor, copywriter, caretaker. He thinks that writing is an irresponsible activity, which releases the gin out of the bottle, while writers are gamblers, untrustworthy jogglers and cooks. As a bilingual person, he appreciates literature that amuses people and moves them.

Karen McPherson is the author of *Skein of Light* (Airlie Press) and the chapbook *Sketching Elise*. Her work has appeared in literary journals including *Beloit Poetry Journal, Cincinnati Review, Potomac Review*, and *Chicago Quarterly Review*. Between 2013 and 2017, she worked as an editor in the Airlie Press poetry collective.

Co-Editor **Miriam Margala** (PhD), a multilingual speaker, dives into all things language. Miriam is fascinated with how people communicate and enjoys immersing into projects that further communication between people, as an educator, a translator, a writer, and an editor. As a literary agent associate, she relishes her role in promoting authors. This special issue, which Miriam edited on request, is a prime example of the type of projects in which she believes.

Erik Markovič (b. 1972) often doesn't know if he is more of a poet, philosopher or a songwriter/musician, so he alternately combines it all into one body of work. Apart from writing poetry, he defined philosophical and aesthetic terms in his post-postmodern manifest, which he had written during the times of peaking postmodernism (2000-2010). His related theory of palintropicity is encompassed in 3 unpublished books. He worked at the Slovak Academy of Sciences in the Philosophical and Encyclopedic Institute. In 2018-2021, he was the Chairman of the Association of Writers' Organizations of Slovakia (AOSS).

Marián Milčák (b. 1960) studied Slovak and German languages and worked as a teacher and a lecturer. His poetic expression is aimed at provoking the reader's thoughts while offering an artistic experience. Memento mori and paraphrases of biblical texts are present in his poetry. He currently teaches at a university in Košice and lives in Levoča.

A graduate in Slovak and English languages, **Peter Milčák** (b. 1966) taught at the secondary level of education before he established his own renowned publishing house Modrý Peter in Levoča, specializing in promoting contemporary Slovak poetry as well as poetry in translation. His own poetics are non-sentimental and philosophical, beautified by metaphors and faith in the good.

Arianna Miller is a poet and educator from Long Island, New York. Her poetry often intermingles nature, generational inheritance, and women's freedom. She received her MFA in poetry from the University of South Carolina and attended the Bread Loaf Writer's Conference as a Poetry Contributor in 2022. Her work has been featured in *Anti-Heroin Chic, Gandy Dancer*, and *The Notre Dame Review*.

Florence Murry is the author of *Last Run Before Sunset*. Her poems have appeared in *Slipstream Press, Blue Earth Review, Wild Roof Journal, Off the Coast, Bluestem Magazine, Westchester Review, Cumberland River Review,* and others. Florence lives in Southern California with her husband and two cats. Her website is https://florencemurrywriter.com.

Erik Ondrejička (b. 1964) attempts to be communicative in his poetry, while striving for aesthetic and ethical quality. He combines a sense of time-transcendence with a contemporary vision of the world. By mastering classical poetic techniques, he seeks to rehabilitate traditional instruments of the poetic art such as rhyme and the music of verse.

A librarian working in Liptovský Mikuláš, **Anna Ondrejková** (b. 1954) has been writing since the 1970s. A poetry for her is not only a state of the world, but also a way of perception. She writes poems to express pain, beauty, and everything in between, while hoping that the human heart can find its relationship to poetry in any era.

Born on Oahu, **Derek N. Otsuji** is the author of *The Kitchen of Small Hours* (SIU Press, 2021), featured in *Honolulu Magazine's* "Essential Hawaii Books You Should Read." He is a 2019 Tennessee Williams Scholar and a 2023 Longleaf Fellow in Poetry. Recent work has appeared in *32 Poems, Southern Review*, and *The Threepenny Review*.

James Owens's newest book is *Family Portrait with Scythe* (Bottom Dog Press, 2020). His poems and translations appear in literary journals, including *Channel, Arc, Dalhousie Review, Queen's Quarterly*, and *The Honest Ulsterman*. He earned an MFA at the University of Alabama and lives in a small town in northern Ontario.

Agda Bavi Pain (b. 1966) is a Slovakian author from Košice. He is a poet, writer, screenwriter, and a frontman of the banned music band Liter Gena. Under several artistic names and brands, Pain has published works in the press, radio, and television in Slovakia as well as abroad. Apart from literature, he also writes for television, film and theatre and has created various TV series, shows and advertising campaigns. Agda Bavi Pain is the co-author of the *European Constitution in Verse* (Brussels, 2009) and he was chosen as one of the seven best Slovak poets after 1989 in a survey in the magazine *Revue of Contemporary Culture*.

As a preacher, **Daniel Pastirčák** (b. 1959) uncovers his spiritual world view in his poems and paintings. A charismatic person and a theological essayist known to a wider public, he considers words of others a building material of his soul and creativity. His personal philosophy is oriented towards high spiritual and esthetic values that are markers of his fine works of art.

Christian Paulisich recently graduated from Johns Hopkins University and reads for *The Hopkins Review*. A Bay Area-native, he currently lives in Baltimore, Maryland. He is a Pushcart Prize nominee whose work can be found in *Literary Matters, Denver Quarterly, New American Writing, Little Patuxent Review*, and others.

Seth Peterson is an emerging writer and physical therapist in Tucson, Arizona. His writing is published or forthcoming in *Bellevue Literary Review, Pirene's Fountain, Santa Fe Literary Review*, and elsewhere. He was a finalist for the 2023 John & Eileen Allman Prize for Poetry and teaches with The Movement Brainery.

Educated as a psychologist, **Dana Podracká** (b. 1954) was employed at the Psychological Institute and as an editor for literary magazines. An important figure in the poetry world, reflecting the depths of women's feelings to the outside world, Dana works at the Slovak Literary Center. Her poetry is full of original images often enhanced by pagan or Christian symbols and historical references. In her words, poetry is a never-ending rite of passage.

Donna Pucciani, a Chicago-based writer, has published poetry in *Shi Chao Poetry, Poetry Salzburg, Journal of the American Medical Association, The Christian Century, ParisLitUp, Gradiva*, and *Atlanta Review*. Her seventh and latest book of poetry is *Edges*.

Justin Pulice is a poet and graduate of the BA Honours English and Creative Writing program at Concordia University. Recently, he has completed his first book of poems, a couple of which will soon appear in *The Antigonish Review* and *Blue Unicorn*. He lives in Montreal with his cat, Kira.

With a doctorate from literary science, **Stanislava Chrobáková Repar** (b. 1960) worked as an editor for Romboid and was a founding member of the Slovak PEN Center. In her research, she examines Slovak poetry of the 20th century and literary hermeneutics. She lives in Slovenia and is works for the Peace Institute in Ljublana, supporting cultural and literary exchange among central European countries.

An editor and a reporter for the magazine Mladá Tvorba, **Peter Repka** (b. 1944) moved to Germany in 1974, and he feels like a domesticated foreigner there and in Slovakia. He is a member of the group of poets Lonely Runners, together with Štrpka and Laučík. In his opinion, poems are not written, but discovered in patient exploration.

Kathy Shorr has lived near the tip of Cape Cod for many years. Poems have appeared in *Prairie Schooner, Quarterly West, Passager, One, The Nebraska Review*, and other journals, and is forthcoming in the *Loch Raven Review*, and has been nominated for Best of the Net.

Caroline N. Simpson's chapbook, *Choose Your Own Adventures and Other Poems*, was published by Finishing Line Press in 2018. In 2020, Delaware Division of Arts awarded Caroline an Established Artist Fellowship in Poetry, and she has been nominated several times for a Pushcart Prize in both poetry and nonfiction. carolinensimpson.com

Jen Siraganian is an Armenian-American writer, educator, and the former Poet Laureate of Los Gatos, California. She has been nominated for a Pushcart Prize and awarded a Lucas Arts Fellowship. Her poetry has appeared or is forthcoming in *Best New Poets, AGNI, Prairie Schooner*, and other journals and anthologies. jensiraganian.com.

Martin Solotruk (b. 1970) has a Ph.D. on American Poetry from the Comenius University, Bratislava, where he now teaches. In his poems, he combines his socialist youth with the vividness of his grandparents' vineyards and a strong sense of the Slavonic Byzantine heritage. He considers the process of writing to be more important than the end product.

Ivan Štrpka (b. 1944) studied Slovak and Spanish languages at the Philosophical Faculty at the Comenius University. An author, whose poetry and prose were not allowed to be published in the 1970s, knows that he exists when he writes. He was the editor in chief for the literary magazine *Romboid* in the years 1999-2010.

Writing prose and poetry, **Peter Šulej** (b. 1967) established a publishing house Drewo a Srd and participated in many literary conferences. For him, poetry expands unclear boundaries by searching for answers. He cannot answer all the questions, but they are sometimes miraculously solved by the readers.

Marilynn Tallal, New York, NY, taught writing for more than forty years from nursery school to college to nursing homes, even a local jail. She won an NEA Creative Writing Fellowship and the Stella Earhart Memorial Award from the University of Houston where she earned the Ph.D. Writing credits include *Poetry, The New Republic, Paris Review, Rattle*, others, and two chapbooks from Presa Press.

Clifford Thompson is the author of five books and the recipient of a Whiting Writers' Award for nonfiction. His essays have appeared in publications including *The Best American Essays 2018*. His poems have been published in *The Georgia Review, Clockhouse, Auburn Avenue, COG magazine*, and *Subnivean*.

Editor Nina Varon, who grew up in Bratislava, lives in Rochester, NY, and works as a language teacher (MSEd) and translator. Spending time with inspiring people and in nature is important to her energy renewal. Seeker of beauty in everyday life, she finds time to paint, sing, and write poems, staying active in like-minded organizations.

Marie Gray Wise's chapbook *Anna and Her Daughters* will be published in 2024 by Finishing Line Press, and she has been nominated by *Naugatuck River Review* for the Best New Poets 2023 anthology. Her work can be found in *Main Street Rag, I-70 Review, Paterson Literary Review*, and at MarieGrayWise.com.

Atlanta Review is indebted to our incredibly generous donors.

For more information about supporting *Atlanta Review,* visit www.atlantareview.com/donate/

If you wish to make a donation to support the journal, please mail a check payable to the **Georgia Tech Foundation**, with *Atlanta Review* on the notes line.

Checks should be mailed to 686 Cherry Street, NW Atlanta, Georgia 30332-0161.

Contributions are tax deductible.

BENEFACTORS

WALT WHITMAN CIRCLE $1,000

ANONYMOUS

KATHY BETTY

DONNA & LARRY BROWN

BOB & JOY DAWSON

ELIZABETH & REID DOWNEY

ELIZABETH S. VALENTINE & ROGER GRIGG

STEVE & PAM HALL

KAREN HEAD & COLIN POTTS

FRIEDA LEVINSKY

TOM & POLLY SAPITOWICZ

SUSAN SHIRLEY & CHRIS SHIRLEY

ALBERT THORNTON

DAN VEACH

Robert Frost Circle $500

Joe & Lisa Bankoff
Henry & Margaret Bourne
Peggy & Robert Dennis
J. H. Grimson
Linda Harris
Ginger Murchison
JC Reilly
Laura Wideburg

Elizabeth Bishop Circle $250

Areatha Anthony • Ruth Blakeney
Gayle Christian • Carole P. Faussemagne
Maggie Hunt-Cohen • Stephen Massimilla
Alvin Pang • Hans Jorg Stahlschmidt
Slobodanka Strauss • Mary Stripling
Lisa Summers • Renata Treitel

Patrons $100

Nina Adlawan • Jacqueline Bardsley
David C. Benton • Steven Ford Brown
Emery L. Campbell • Robert Champ
Tom Chandler • Stephanie Kaplan Cohen
Catherine Colinvaux • Liz & Tom Cooksey
Barbara Clark • John Crawford
Terry Hensel • Ruth Kinsey
Joan Kunsch • Gloria Lewyn
Lee & Candace Passarella • Wanda Praisner
Ron Self • John Stephens • Bert Thornton
Jim Tilley • Stephen & Ruth Windham
Ellen & Dan Zegura

Donors $50

Joe Bankoff • Dorothy Brooks • John O. Connell
Barbara Lydecker Crane • Peter Fontaine
Rebecca Foust • Dr. Edda H. Hackl
David & Christy Hand
Sandra K. Kennedy • Jay Kidd
Ed & Sylvia Krebs • Marjorie Mir
Janet Murray • Dean Olson
Korkut Onaran • Sherman Pearl
Diane Powell • Carol Senf
Peter Serchuk • Leslie Sharp
Michael Spence • Alicia Stallings • Brad Vickers
Jennifer Wheelock • Tonia Williams
David Zoll • Wanita Zumbrunnen

Friends $30

William I. Allgood • Diana Anhalt
Rebecca Baggett • Virginia Beards
Jesse Bodley • Ronald Boggs
Gaylord Brewer • Bette Callahan
Robin S. Chapman • Shannon Dobranski
Mary Dowd • Booky Ellis
Catlyn Fendler • Karie Friedman
Steven Girardot • Rachel Hadas
Amy Henry • Mary Anderson Hill
Sandra Larson • Donald Lashley
Charles Liverpool • Perie Longo
Kay O'Connell • Maribeth Price
Lee Rossi • Andrew Schillinger
Wanita A. Zumbrunnen

POETRY

Annual International Poetry Competition

Grand Prize
$1,000

25 International Publication Prizes
Publication in the Fall issue of Atlanta Review

30 International Merit Awards
List of honor in Atlanta Review, *free contest issue*

Easy Online Entry:

https://atlantareview.submittable.com/

Submission Dates: February 1-May 1